Outside the Not So Big House

Outside the Not So Big House

Creating the Landscape of Home

Julie Moir Messervy
and Sarah Susanka

Photographs by
Grey Crawford

The Taunton Press

The Taunton Press
Inspiration for hands-on living®

The Taunton Press, Inc., 63 South Main Street, PO Box 5506, Newtown, CT 06470-5506
e-mail: tp@taunton.com

Outside the Not So Big House was originally published in 2006 in hardcover by The Taunton Press, Inc.

Editor: Erica Sanders-Foege
Jacket/Cover design: Alexander Isley, Inc.
Interior design and layout: Carol Petro
Illustrator: Christine Erikson
Photographer: Grey Crawford

LIBRARY OF CONGRESS CATALOGING-IN-PUBLICATION DATA
Messervy, Julie Moir.
  Outside the not so big house : creating the landscape of home / Julie Moir Messervy and Sarah Susanka ;
photographs by Grey Crawford.
      p. cm.
ISBN-13: 978-1-56158-734-6 hardcover
ISBN-10: 1-56158-734-6 hardcover
ISBN-13: 978-1-60085-020-2 paperback (with flaps)
 1. Landscape gardening. 2. Gardens--Philosophy. 3. Architecture, Domestic. I. Susanka, Sarah. II. Crawford, Grey. III.
Title.
 SB473.M447 2006
 712'.6--dc22
                                    2005018828

Printed in Thailand
10 9 8 7 6 5 4 3 2 1

Acknowledgments

Writing a book is a lot like designing a garden: You seek to understand the elements involved, construct a frame in which to work, weave the parts together, and craft the details to get them right. Throughout, you need to return to the material time and again with fresh eyes.

Everyone who worked with me on this book has fresh eyes. Sarah is an articulate and tireless advocate for good design, using all her senses to express so eloquently what she sees and how to make it better. Seeing the world through Grey Crawford's camera lens as he photographed these properties was a privilege. Underneath his signature fedora is a pair of hawk eyes and fierce intellect that combine with a fine sense of humor and an easygoing working style. Executive Editor Maureen Graney helped me in the early stages to conceptualize the book and organize it properly. Editor Erica Sanders-Foege then took the editorial reins and guided me through its writing. With her incisive intelligence and dry humor, she sharpened and simplified my writing and helped teach me the Taunton way. Publisher Jim Childs and editor-in-chief Maria Taylor saw the possibilities in combining Sarah's and my visions. Art director Paula Schlosser's ability to graphically express the layout made it real for me from the start; design manager Carol Singer fine-tuned the design so that it flows.

Of course, many others played a part in making this book happen. I owe thanks to my literary agent, Christina Ward for her clear perspective and support; to my colleague, landscape architect Ed Hartranft, for his effervescent brilliance as a form-giver; and to landscape designer Amanda Sloan, who supports our design work with good humor, patience, and constant creativity. Virginia Small, who suggested my name to the Taunton book division, continues to shepherd me through the writing of my columns. I am grateful to all of these wonderful friends for their consistent support of my ideas.

And finally, I want to thank my family: my children, Max, Lindsey, and Charlotte, and my stepson, Luke; my parents, William and Alice Moir, and my sisters and brothers—you know who you are! I am lucky to be so loved. And with my soul mate, Steve Jonas at my side, I feel truly blessed.

– Julie

Contents

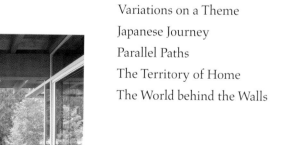

Julie's Preface

I've been designing, as well as thinking, talking, and writing about landscapes, for thirty years now; actually a lot longer if you include my delight in the world of nature as a child. I've developed my own landscape design theories in three published books, including *The Inward Garden*, and I continue to hone my design skills on projects that range from home landscapes to cemeteries, museum gardens, and campus master plans. I owe much to the mentors who have helped me along my journey. Many years ago, the late eminent Japanese garden master Kinsaku Nakane taught me the art of Japanese garden design, whose principles form the heart this book. My graduate training at MIT's School of Architecture gave me a background in design theory and building practice that continues to be vital to my understanding of home design. Renowned cellist Yo-Yo Ma brought me to the city of Toronto to design the three-acre Toronto Music Garden that is based on the *First Suite for Unaccompanied Cello* by J. S. Bach. His delight in fueling creative collaborations and in finding connections between the different arts continues to inspire and challenge me to "hear the stream with open eyes."

In this book, I join forces with another visionary, Sarah Susanka. As landscape designer and architect, we make a good team. From our different perspectives, Sarah and I craft a language that speaks to the heart of design and gives our readers the ability to "listen" to their environment from a spatial point of view. Together, we seek to explain through words, photographs, and drawings how and why good design works for us all, so that we can better attune our properties to fit our needs. Sarah and I hope that this book will make the fields of landscape and architectural design more accessible to those who weren't trained in the field, while encouraging homeowners, builders, developers, real estate agents, and design professionals to converse more fluently with each other about the characteristics of home and land. Just as we've done by working together on this book, we hope to break down the barriers between design professions through the conceptual language we use to explain the inspiring examples of good landscape and architectural design in this book. *Outside the Not So Big House* is, in essence, a photographic dictionary of ideas to help readers understand their surroundings in a whole new way.

—Julie

Sarah's Preface

Home describes so much more than just the structure we live in. It also includes the land that surrounds the structure. Home is the entire dwelling place, inside and out. In fact, the Japanese have an ideogram— a kanji—that perfectly depicts this understanding of home. It is composed of two parts—the symbol for house and the symbol for garden. The two together form the kanji that in Japanese is pronounced *katei*.

I'm able to articulate this concept but, because I'm not trained in landscape design, I haven't ever felt confident enough to illustrate it. Julie, on the other hand, has the knowledge and the eloquence to explain the qualities of outside spaces that are needed to truly realize what *katei* is all about. I realized immediately that if she'd be willing to collaborate on a book about the outside part of what *katei* means, then we'd have a very powerful message to relate.

Julie's and my experiences have been similar and our understandings about how space is experienced are almost perfectly parallel. We have been deeply influenced by *A Pattern Language*, by Christopher Alexander et al., which was published in 1977, when we were each in school, and we have had an abiding interest in Japanese design. Julie, in the midst of her architectural training, studied with a garden master in Kyoto. Over the year and a half she spent there, she learned the art of garden composition and, on her return, began to build, teach, and write about landscape design.

My architectural education took me to Japan as well. Though my trip was just a few weeks in length, I learned an enormous amount, more than books could teach me, about the power of spatial experience. The trip also convinced me that the exterior surroundings of a house—or any building for that matter—are just as important as the interior. I knew that for my message about smaller, better-designed houses to be complete, I needed to find a way to illustrate this, and Julie's collaboration is the first step in that direction.

That said, this book is *not* only about landscaping or gardening. It's about the transitions and connections between the inside of a house and the outside, and about the journeys and the places that can be made to extend the experience of home to the outside. Just as the inside of a house is a sequence of places for the experiences of daily life, so the outside continues this sequence. And the paths and places along the way, whether inside, outside, or in the in-between zone, are together what we call *home*. I hope you'll enjoy this extension of the Not So Big message. Whatever the size of your property, the ideas contained herein will help to make your house and garden two parts of a singular whole—your very own *katei*.

—Sarah

The Landscape of Home

My starter home was a big Victorian on a tiny site in a neighborhood of Boston. With its wraparound porch, turret, and stained-glass windows, it was an exciting house for bringing up a family. But when I ask my children about this period, they describe how they used the landscape, making cascades over the backyard ledges with the hose, building forts in the forsythia bush, and conducting tea parties on the steps of the front porch. Creating these spaces for outdoor living brought us as much—if not more—pleasure as decorating the inside because we were using the outside as an extension of our house. And by extending the house, we transformed the whole property into what I call our landscape of home.

Each of us carries a mental picture of what constitutes our particular landscape of home. It might be entertaining friends for dinner under a grape arbor or roasting marshmallows around a firepit or perching on a parapet looking out to a distant view. Gardens are also part of the landscape of home. A cottage garden greets visitors from the street. A water garden brings sound and visual delight to a corner of the yard. As a landscape designer, I work closely with my clients to wrest these images from them so that I can design gardens that match their inner visions.

Not So Big refers to an attitude rather than the size of a house. In this book, we are not addressing just those with a modest piece of land, but those with properties that range from a 10th of an acre to 100 acres. Not So Big refers to houses that don't overwhelm the size of the lot but allow plenty of "breathing room" around it for growing, for entertaining, or for contemplation. Not So Big suggests a way of crafting your house so that it feels like home and crafting your property so that you feel at home on your land. This usually means creating a house about one-third smaller than you thought you needed.

Most homeowners are overwhelmed by the vast amount of information required to know how to organize their space into a coherent whole. Often, they have no idea where to begin. Perhaps it is because, unlike the inside of a house where each room has walls, a ceiling, and a floor, the outside feels boundless, and little but the property line is defined.

And the possibilities seem limitless, bounded only by one's budget, which is usually constrained after the expenses of building or renovating. So the question is: How do we make the outside of our homes as wonderful as the inside? How can we craft places on the land that fulfill our needs and delight our souls? In *Outside the Not So Big House*, you'll find the answers as we break down this new design territory, the landscape of home.

In her earlier Not So Big books, Sarah explained how to make a house into a home. Giving words to spatial concepts that underlie

> **Using framed openings is one way to link inside to outside. Double doors frame a view to the brick terrace, surrounded by flowers that seem to tumble down the hillside.**

our understanding of the built environment, she developed a language of space and form that describes the qualitative experience that people want in a house. As they read her books, many asked for help in thinking about how to approach the landscape from a Not So Big perspective. In this book, we do just that, for we believe that a house is not a home unless it is seamlessly interconnected with the landscape around it.

∧ Working outside a house requires a close relationship between designer and client. Here, carefully applied native materials contribute to the impression that this Colorado home is growing right up out of the site.

Imagine a house where you throw open the doors to find an outdoor world in which you can live with all the comforts of home. What would this look like? Just as in the inside, you would have areas of "shelter around activity," such as the grape arbor, where you sit in a protected place looking out onto a larger space beyond. You'd find the Not So Big concept of "layering," in which a series of openings and surfaces break the perceived space into segments, as when sliding doors open out to a veranda that flows down to a series of terraces beyond. And you'd find at least one "away room," such as a cozy gazebo that provides sanctuary. As you'll learn, many Not So Big concepts also apply to outside spaces, helping to connect the inside of your home to the landscape around it.

A New Definition of Home
What do we mean by the landscape of home? It's not only the gardens, but also the views and vistas, and the walkways and thresholds that let you feel at home on your land. Of course, your house is part of this landscape, too. How do you decide when to use these elements? You begin by realizing that designing your landscape is not so different from designing your house. Each property in the chapters that follow shows a different response to the challenges posed by site and structure, but the professionals who designed the properties used similar tools to create very different landscapes. Giving names to those conceptual

∧ A bronze water feature echoes the forms of adjacent tree trunks and brings gentle sounds to this sylvan place. Mossy stones are carefully set to make the artificial pond feel natural.

We typically discuss landscaping as though it were something completely separate from the house. If you look at most garden design, you'll be hard pressed to find much connection between inside and out. There might be a screened porch, a terrace, or a deck that provides a gesture at a transition between inside and out. But there's often nothing else.

Like the artistry required in designing a welcoming entrance, there's an artistry required in the design of the interconnections between interior and exterior places. There's much potential to enhance the experience of everyday living when you consider the outdoors as a design element of the indoor space. And vice versa.

Every interior sitting space and activity area offers the opportunity to connect to and participate in a particular aspect of the surrounding landscape, whether that be a view to a beautiful tree, a long vista to a standing stone at the far corner of the property, or a glimpse through a tiny window to a courtyard garden. When inside and outside are designed as one, the results can inspire you on a daily basis, feeding your spirit and allowing you to truly delight in the natural world without having to go outside to do so.   *—Sarah*

< The approach to your property sets the tone for the experience of entering the house. Here, a gravel driveway brings visitors to a garden court before they cross the threshold.

tools—i.e., the language of the landscape of home—is the first step in understanding the design process so that you can use them to create your own.

Site
Embracing the Habitat of Home

Your site, your house, and your outbuildings make up your habitat: the environment where you feel most at home. When you create the right habitat of home, you set the table for all other design decisions. Every site has a vantage: either a prospect—a view from a high position, as on a mountain; or a refuge—a protected setting such as under a canopy of trees. To create the most favorable setting, it's important to know how the site is oriented, its soils, and existing vegetation. Your house also enjoys a particular relationship to the land, with slopes that face upward, downward, or remain level. Those familiar with Not So Big principles

∧ The vantage of a warm hot tub is perfect for taking in the mountain view.

> From the dining room, the high windows create the feeling of sitting in a terrarium.

> Ground covers and perennials tumble down the hillside, drenching a stone retaining wall in soft textures and colors. The simplicity of the house stands up well to the garden, which is bursting with plants.

will see the connection. Like a home designed for the way we really live, a landscape designed to make the most of its site is more inspiring and more fitting.

One property in the book, a Not So Big House set high in the Berkeley Hills, was designed to take advantage of every square inch of its narrow site. The house nestles into a steep slope and, in every room, high-framed windows and doors bring in views of a flower garden that was lovingly planted by the owners. Brick and stone terraces offer places for entertaining and quiet contemplation, helping make this the perfect habitat for the social couple who live here.

Flow
Composing Journeys

Stripped down to its essentials, a landscape is really composed of two elements: paths and places. A path indicates the way you should flow through a landscape—which direction to stroll in and the pace you walk—as well as the mood with which you move.

∧ The water garden is a terminus for one journey on this property.

> This stepping-stone path winds through beds of hosta and underneath the shade of a magnolia tree, linking front yard to back.

∧ A path of flat fieldstone brings the visitor to a curved retaining wall—an overlook and place to sit that invites body and mind to rest a while.

Places are stopping points you encounter along the way, such as spaces for enjoying views inside and outside the house. You can choreograph movement through space, from place to place, through the design of the journey that the path takes. Like a Not So Big house that has a thoughtful circulation pattern that leads us through the entire house, a landscape with a carefully designed journey is one that integrates the inside flow to the outside and vice versa. Whether meandering or straight, a well-designed path links different places, events, or activities to each other around our properties.

The rocky stream that flows alongside one house in the book leads visitors from the cobbled parking court across a bridge to a roofed outdoor veranda. The veranda follows the meandering streambed and terminates in a circular outdoor room that overlooks the water. Sitting in what is a private escape for this in-town house, visitors can enjoy the sight and sounds of the babbling watercourse.

Frames
Linking the Inside With the Out

It's wonderful to look out the windows of your house and see a landscape that knits nature and building into one complete design. Your home feels as though it extends beyond the walls of the house.

Being mindful of framed openings, such as windows and doors, helps you to establish a visual link between inside and out. In addition, building transitional spaces, like decks, porches, or balconies, makes the space between building and landscape more accessible. By enclosing parts of the landscape with walls, fences, or hedges, you create outdoor rooms as pleasing as those inside the house. When you create frames—structures that surround or enclose a particular space—you extend the presence of home beyond your house to embrace the whole property. Of course, this very concept of indoor-outdoor connection is at the heart of Not So Big design.

Λ This framed opening looks out on a lovely garden scene: a pool graced by a grove of bamboo.

< The front porch with its red butterfly chairs looks out upon the neighborhood. A simple tin roof tops the ipé deck, providing needed shade in the Texas heat.

∨ This Chicago garden is crafted from inexpensive materials but planted with a rich palette and a deft hand.

A Not So Big House in Texas displays many ways to link inside to outside. With an open floor plan that maximizes every bit of space, the house features floor-to-ceiling windows that offer views out to the backyard. A deck seems to float over a series of lawn panels that step down to the level yard. The owners are free to live equally inside or outside on their property, experiencing every inch of their landscape of home.

Details

Crafting the Elements of Nature

You craft the inside of your home when you choose a window style or a special molding. Each selection reflects your style and displays aspects of your personality, as an individual, a couple, or a family. Similarly, the details that you choose in crafting your outdoor landscape help to anchor the house to its surrounds. This means emphasizing the interplay of materials and echoing forms and patterns to bring consistency to the whole. For example, you can compose a planting palette using colors and textures that

∧ **An inveterate gardener planted a wide range of trees, shrubs, and perennials in her front yard and painted the porch columns bright yellow.**

delight. Or select native materials that suggest a sense of the history of your locale. By shaping the personality of your home this way, you bring outside into union with inside. And whether or not you're talking about the interior of your home or the area surrounding it, all good design comes down to the crafting of the details.

Every property in this book possesses elegantly crafted details, but one Chicago residence shows how effective using simple building materials with beautiful plantings can be. Carefully edged planting beds harness riots of colors and textures. Each detail fits into the whole; the whole is defined by the personality and aesthetic of the owner.

Owning the Landscape
As you read through this book, you'll discover new ideas and images that will indelibly change the way you see—and own—your property. Look out your kitchen window, and you'll imagine a host of new possibilities: a wildflower meadow or a deck floating over a lily pond. You'll learn techniques for designing an appealing approach to your home, methods for making a small property seem bigger, and ways to hide views and reveal others. The variety of land-scapes and houses highlighted in this book—large and small, located in rural, suburban, or urban settings all around the country—offer ample ideas for every homeowner.

In the simplest sense, the ideas in this book are all about well-being: being well both in your house and on your land. Isn't this what we all want from our homes? Just as my children took delight in playing in spaces we made for them outside our house, so too will you derive joy from creating your own very personal landscape of home.

Site

Site

Embracing the Habitat of Home

The features that make a site special
create a unique and distinctive landscape,
both inside and out.

A screened room sits at a prime location for viewing down the valley to the Vermont mountains beyond. Notice how the local slate under the deep eaves of the veranda matches the gray-green color of the standing-seam roof.

Playing Up the Corners

I t's thrilling to see the elegance and beauty of Sarah's Not So Big principles come to life in this home for a retired couple near Stowe, Vermont. Sited on a large piece of land, the residence sits in a lovely garden and looks out upon a majestic view. The property, a west-facing meadow reminiscent of the former farm community of north central Vermont, is located high up on Elmore Mountain and faces west, looking across to a distant Mount Mansfield. The owners, returning to their Vermont roots, looked to Sarah and landscape designer Cynthia Knauf to design a home with a strong indoor-outdoor connection through a composition of pattern, detail, and scale. Their love of Prairie-style architecture and the Japanese aesthetic supports the design of the house and land to express a harmony between their lifestyle and the natural surroundings.

NOT SO BIG INSIDE OUT

Situated on a beautiful piece of Vermont mountainside, this home is designed to extend its apparent territory all the way to the horizon. Intended to encourage the use of its many outdoor spaces whenever the weather allows, house and land interweave to create a series of spatial layers from interior, to a space I call "beneath the roof but outside," to garden. The sequence of places that connects them makes a continuous necklace around and through the house, and it's this collection that creates the feeling of home.
          —*Sarah*

The old farm road to the house climbs steadily through a meadow of lupine, daisies, black-eyed Susans, and asters. Designed as a series of horizontal planes, the low-slung structure, with green metal roofs, a massive stone chimney, and an attached garage, sits on garden terraces that ease into the wildflower meadow. A gentle arc in the driveway brings visitors to the front walk. A ribbon of bluestone moves them past a natural stone water basin scooped out to collect rainwater. Here, a transverse path of flat fieldstone interrupts the cut-stone walkway, offering viewers a tempting walk around the garden before entering the house. This path winds through native plantings and past the occasional boulder before ending up at a small Vermont slate terrace at the corner of the house.

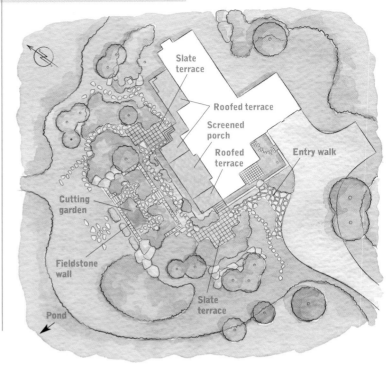

Slate terrace

Roofed terrace

Screened porch

Roofed terrace

Entry walk

Cutting garden

Fieldstone wall

Slate terrace

Pond

> A swimming pond reflects the silhouettes of trees and the lights of this handsome home in Vermont.

∨ This natural fieldstone, found on the property, was hollowed out as an "event" along the walk to the front door, perhaps a reference to the placement of *tsukubai*—a water basin along a Japanese tea garden path.

∧ The use of local materials relates this house wonderfully to its surrounds. The front walk interweaves several kinds of stones to help signal which way to go: Take the straight, cut-stone walkway to get to the front door, or follow the irregular stepping-stone path to stroll around the garden.

Corners Indoors and Out

Both architect and landscape architect play up the corners of this home: Sarah, by placing a bank of windows that wraps around the corner, makes the wall seem to disappear and frames the views so that inside and outside are one. She also placed a window seat that beckons one to sit and linger, looking out to the garden and beyond. By featuring the corners of a space, Sarah makes the space feel bigger than it really is, drawing the eye across the room and to the views.

The same is true outside the house as well. By drawing feet and eyes to the corners of the upper terraces just outside the screened porch, the landscape designer expanded the virtual frame around the house. She also made a place for the corner of the house by creating a void of space that accepts and defuses the corner's energy. Backing up the table and chairs that sit at the outer edge of the terrace with a weeping larch tree, shrubs, and flowering perennials, she echoed the idea behind the window seat, allowing visitors to inhabit the corner of the garden.

At the northern side of the landscape, the designer added another slate terrace, this time as a backdrop for a set of steps that cascade down from the corner of the slate walkway, which unites screened porch and upper terrace. Here, visitors are greeted by a series of offset rectangles that are emphasized by the shape of the teak benches. Stepping-stones, planted on a gravel path that tunnels through soft drifts of plantings, offer a way down to the pond.

Framing the View

Sitting at the western edge of the house, the screened porch looks out across terraces and pond to the setting sun over Mount Mansfield. The vista unfolds like a Japanese screen, segmented into 12 separate aspects of the same scene: The lower band of four "frames" looks onto the terrace, the middle set focuses on views across the pond, and the top four define the sky. The curving roofline and the upper clerestory also allow for views of the sky; where the window arcs downward, it pulls the eye back into the forest that surrounds the whole property.

From within the house, you have views through interior doorways and windows, so inside and outside continually overlap. An interior eyebrow window lets light into the room, echoed again in the wood fireplace frame. With vistas like these, it pays to "borrow" them, bringing them into your living space by framing each view like the work of art it is.

∧ The view from the screened porch looks across layers of landscape: over a stepping-stone terrace to a cutting garden, across pond and fields and forest to the mountains in the distance. The raised eyebrow window gives unfettered views to the sky.

< Washed pea gravel is the ground cover in this section of the garden, where a layer of landscape fabric has been laid to keep the weeds from cropping up.

∨ Sarah echoed the eyebrow form seen above the screened porch in various places around the house. The curved motif is carried above the fireplace and the clerestory window above the door in the away room.

A Base of Support

To feel rooted to the ground and promote flow between inside and outside, a house needs a solid and level base of support. The way I think about this is to imagine that the house has fallen forward onto its front façade. The area left by its imprint is about the right amount of level ground needed for a good base of support. This area might be taken up by a series of terraces that step downhill, as at this house, or by one level space for patio, garden, or lawn in front of the house.

I think of this as the "aura" of the house, displaced onto the land. Landscape designer Cynthia Knauf furthers the idea of the house projected onto the land by echoing the curve of the eyebrow window on the porch in her cobble design on the ground. The base of support for the house steps out and down the slope by the creation of a lower terrace, retained by a handsome fieldstone wall. Here, Cynthia designed a cutting garden composed of annuals and perennials planted for flower arrangements created by the owner.
                                                                    —Julie

Blurring the Boundary

SARAH'S LOW-SLUNG roofs create a transitional space under the eaves that acts like a porch, a terrace, and a front stoop all in one. Since the roof doesn't have gutters, she provides a drip line of Mexican beach pebbles that sit in a trough formed by the curb that bounds the driveway and the concrete floor of the area under the eaves.

This drip line further defines the aura of the house; its straight lines set it apart from the natural landscape while its contents—the black beach stones—relate to the bluestone walkway that leads you into the house. The massive wooden pillar that holds up the corner of the house sits on a flat fieldstone base, further blurring the boundaries between house and garden, inside and out.   —*Julie*

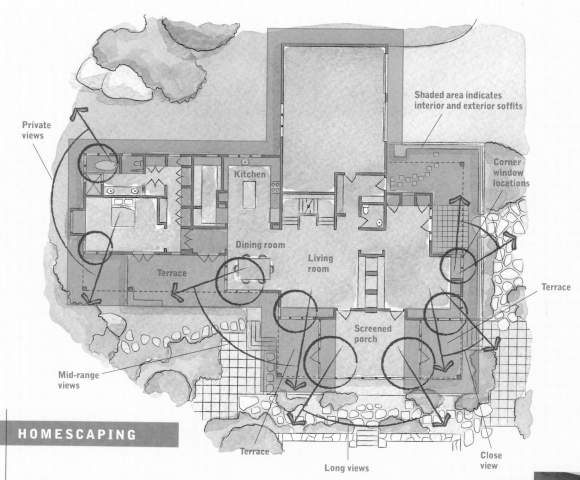

Private views

Shaded area indicates interior and exterior soffits

Corner window locations

Kitchen

Dining room

Living room

Terrace

Mid-range views

Terrace

Screened porch

Terrace

Long views

Close view

HOMESCAPING

Corner Windows

In designing this house, I wanted to give the homeowners the sense, from every major room, that they were all but outside. One of the best ways I've found to achieve this is to "erode" the solidity of the corners so that you are able to look through the part of the house that we most associate with structure and stability. Not only does this increase the view, but it also encourages you to inhabit the corners. A corner, even one that's not wrapped with windows, will provide a sense of shelter for any activity located there. But when there is a series of windows on either side of the corner post, the appeal of inhabiting the corner becomes hard to resist.

The window seat shown here is further enhanced by the lowered ceiling, which, like the kitchen soffit described at right, provides shelter around the activity of sitting and gazing at the view, reading a book, or just daydreaming.

Like the soffit in the kitchen, the eaves beyond the windows are the same height as the lowered ceiling, giving the impression that the boundary created by the windows is only a minimal obstacle between you and the surrounding landscape. Notice that the peeled-log post supporting the roof that extends out over the adjacent terrace aligns with the window mullions as well. This further blurs the distinction between what's inside and what's out.

Looking at the floor plan, you'll see that there are similar sitting places in the living room and dining room, as well as in one of the guest bedrooms on the second floor. The screened porch takes this attitude of the eroded corner to its logical extreme. In a way, the room is all open corners, with no solid wall left at all, yet there's still protection supplied by the roof above. It's one of the reasons I believe people enjoy screened porches so much. There's protection, but only a minimal boundary between inside and out.

—Sarah

Blurring the Boundary

JUST AS the wide overhangs give a sense of protection on the exterior, on the interior lots of dropped ceilings over window seats and above countertops help give a sense of shelter to the activity places below. For example, I lowered the ceiling to the height of the window trim above the kitchen sink, so that when working here, a person is not only connected to the view, but also feels protected from above, much as how one feels when wearing a wide-brimmed hat. The eaves are at the same height as the dropped ceiling within, so it appears that the wide brim extends from inside to out. With the extension of the windows all the way to the countertop, the boundary created by the wall is minimized. *—Sarah*

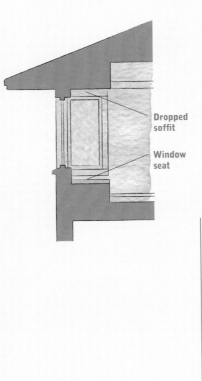

Dropped soffit

Window seat

Sarah has designed a wonderful perching place that feels like part of house and landscape at the same time. A gray slate veranda sits 2 ft. above the garden level, protected under deep eaves. Steps that flow from its interior corner lead down to a red slate terrace, where stepping stones lead out to the natural landscape beyond.

1	2	3
4	5	6
7	8	9

5 **The bonsai trees** are members of the client's collection: one a diminutive Japanese maple and the other a white pine—a miniature of the weeping white pine that towers above it.

6 **Billowing plantings** of different heights, colors, and textures are carefully pruned to allow views out, yet they create the feeling of an enclosed garden within. Mount Mansfield peeks out over the autumnal colors of maple trees in the near distance.

3 **The client asked** the landscape designer to make a maintenance notebook that explains what to do with every plant in her garden. Here, the flowering stages for the meadow for spring and summer were documented before it was cut back in the fall.

One of the delights of living in a colder climate is enjoying the different seasons. In the crisp fall air, maple trees turn brilliant colors before losing their leaves.

White roses—"Prosperity" on the left and "Ballerina" on the
right—stand out vividly against the deep, soft greens of the garden
plantings. A brick path flows around the stucco walls of the house.

Borrowing the Landscape

I magine a charming little house with a private backyard that
nestles into a hillside of flowers with a view to a city skyline in
the distance. This combination of contemplative remove and
vibrant accessibility perfectly describes this sliver of property in the
Berkeley Hills in California. Located on a steep hill, this "walk-to"
parcel is accessed only by a public pathway—a narrow, flower-strewn
lane that ascends through steeply banked retaining walls as a series
of steps and landings.

At the top of a set of stairs, a metal gate arches out into the public
path announcing the entrance. Two sharp rights and a left-hand turn
bring visitors to the front door. The home's close proximity to the
public walkway, combined with its circuitous means of access, under-
scores a delightful tension between nearness and farness; between
remove and accessibility.

NOT SO BIG INSIDE OUT

Some properties, like this tiny but delightful California
home, have a topography to them that says "shelter," whether
you are talking about the house, the land, or both in combination. This one has an archetypal "nestled" quality to it resulting
from the shape of the surrounding landscape, a quality that
both architect and landscape architect have capitalized upon
to make the home a lush, green, and secluded paradise from
every vantage point.

—Sarah

∧ **Visitors pass cascading nasturtium blossoms and bamboo rising against the retaining walls before they reach the beckoning gate and trellis.**

Architect Dennis Fox renovated this diminutive home, built in the 1930s, from a tiny 918 sq. ft. to a still-modest 1,084 sq. ft. To take advantage of the views of the landscape offered by the steep hillside in the back, he placed the private rooms—the master bedroom, kitchen, and dining room—on the garden side of the house. Looking from slope down to house, the structure is a stucco box that stands in stark contrast to the flow of the landscape. But when one looks from the inside out, something magical happens: It feels as though all distinctions between house and garden have disappeared, almost like one is inside a terrarium. The architect created this effect by lowering windowsills and doorsills (to better merge with the landscape) and by heightening ceilings in order to include banks of

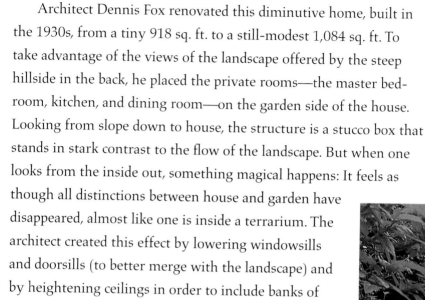

∨ **Roses open to the sun in this exuberantly planted backyard garden—a pleasing contrast to the spare interior rooms of the house.**

ALL AROUND THE HOUSE

Planted slope

"Borrowed landscape"

Brick walkway

Entry gate

Public walkway

Entry gate

Entry porch

Skyline view

Stone terrace

clerestory windows above vertical fixed and casement windows. The clerestories open up the view to the top of the hill with tree ferns, rose blossoms, and billowing shrubs that spill down the slope, and the lowered windowsills bring foreground plantings right into the house.

A Borrowed Landscape
The living room lies on the western side of the property, facing the setting sun and San Francisco Bay. As you enter, your eye is drawn to a single doorway onto a balcony with a view across the neighbor's roof to the distant skyline. Here, the architect employed a Japanese gardening

∧ The architect lowered the doorsill so that the terrace level appears to sweep right in the door. This effect is furthered by the plantings at the threshold and the foundation line of the house.

> Sheltered by the sloping hillside, this teak bench and chair offer a tempting spot for contemplation. The stockade fence, drenched in vines, may define the property line between houses, but it doesn't stop the eye from "borrowing" the neighbor's view.

∨ Tree ferns grow on the slope above the house like a forest primeval. Narrow mulched trails traverse the hillside, terminating in a solitary bench or chair.

technique called *shakkei,* or "borrowing the landscape." Fox called attention to the best vista on the property by erecting a kind of vertical picture frame around it. The door casing borders the top and sides of the picture plane, and a dense hedge and neighboring trees further intensify the view. The distant view within the small frame is a surprising and satisfying visual experience. It also acts as a reminder of this home's relationship with the city: The city feels close enough to "borrow," yet its scale is small enough to give a sense of vast distance.

Landscape architect Heather Anderson chose to literally borrow the neighbor's landscape in her design of this backyard garden. Her planting plan encompassed the mature trees on and adjacent to

< Planting up against the foundation of a house can make it feel as though it springs forth from a garden. Otherwise, a garden can seem like an afterthought. Soft euphorbias contrast with spiky agaves in the afternoon sun.

Upward-Facing Slopes

This property sits on the terraced shelf just below a steeply sloping hillside. Thus, the backyard looks directly into the bank of what I call an upward-facing slope. This condition allows intimate views of a landscape, which is seen as a flipped-up plane, like a huge landscape canvas propped up on an easel. What delights here is that every inch of hillside becomes valuable, for it not only makes up the view from within the house but also the enclosure that forms the backyard, while offering secret trails and contemplative perches for solitary strollers. An upward-facing slope turns into a downward-facing one when these vantage points high on the hill become places

to pause and literally reflect on where you came from, or where you're planning to go.

—*Julie*

the site, creating the sense that the property continues beyond its actual boundaries. Concrete-rubble retaining walls were used to make a small cut into the hillside to gain areas for seating. Brick and stone pathways surround the building, opening up to create terraces and, paradoxically, encouraging close-up scrutiny of the voluptuous plantings all around.

< The hillside of flowers seems to cascade right into the wraparound windows of this Not So Big dining room. Clerestory windows allow a view up the slope and into branches overhead.

Sense of Shelter

IN THE VAST expanses of the great outdoors, we seek out places of shelter, precincts where we feel protected and secure while being able to survey the landscape around us. We seek a strong "back" to nestle against—such as a hillside—some kind of enclosing arms that harbor and enfold while allowing for a view out.

Landscape architect Heather Anderson placed a teak bench on its own small terrace, backed up against the upward-facing slope of plantings, where it looks out and down to the view beyond. Here, the space is private as well as protected from winds from the San Francisco Bay. The stone steps entice us to ascend, look around, and smell the roses.   *—Julie*

Window Positioning

We've all been in houses in which you are cut off from the surrounding views the moment you sit down. There's nothing more frustrating than knowing there's a beautiful view beyond the window but being unable to see it because the windowsill is too high. The architect for this home has been careful to make windowsills in the dining room and bedroom about 24 in. off the floor so that, as you sit at the dining table or lie in bed, you can easily see out and down a bit as well.

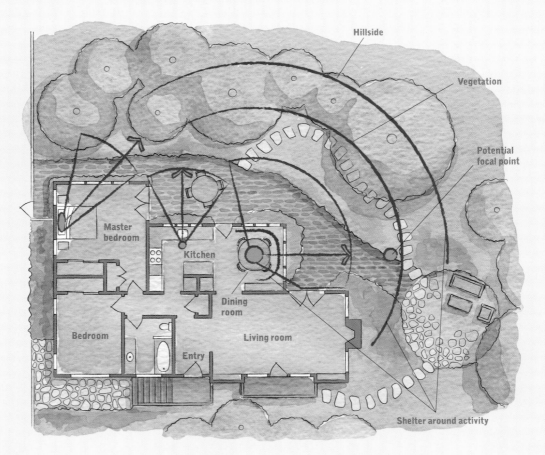

The same is true for the kitchen, but here the sill height must be appropriately scaled for someone standing at the countertop. Here again, the architect has made the backsplash a minimal 2½ in., so as you stand at the sink, you feel very much a part of the outdoor space. As you can see in the doctored image (below, left), a higher sill gives much more of a sense of separation.

Windows can provide a geometrical patterning for interior space as well. Notice how, with the windows in the dining room, our focus is drawn to the larger middle windowpane. This is because the smaller surrounding windows serve as a frame. Although they contain views of their own, they delineate the point of focus for the whole room. For this reason, the place in the garden to where your attention is drawn might also be the spot for a special feature, such as a fountain, a wonderful stone, or a plant. It's this integration between inside and out that really weaves the two into an integrated whole.   *—Sarah*

Shelter Around Activity

JULIE HAS DESCRIBED how the shape of the surrounding hill can give the sense of shelter. At the entrance, below, the slope's presence is comforting. But perhaps the place where we're most familiar with this sense is in the corner of a room. Why else do you think it is that the corner tables and booths in a restaurant are always the most prized spots? We tend to seek out the corners because we feel more protected, and so more comfortable.

As you look at the dining-room corner, you'll see that there's the shelter provided by the hill and its plantings. The nestled feeling you get while sitting here is palpable. You are doubly sheltered, and so doubly comfortable.   *—Sarah*

The Attraction of Opposites

Our homes often reflect a particular view of our place in the continuum between the built environment and the world of nature. Frank and Judy Harmon's house in Raleigh, North Carolina, is no different. It's designed to mirror and attract oppositions between inside and out, hard and soft, light and dark, and private and public. Pooling their respective design talents—as architect and landscape architect—the couple created a wonderfully livable home that instructs as much as it inspires.

When they bought a derelict piece of land in a university neighborhood of Raleigh more than a decade ago, Judy and Frank studied the site for a year before sketching out a series of schemes. In order to create the largest garden space possible, they ended up building an elegant boxlike house of concrete, steel, and glass that sits at the back of the property. To counter the noise of student life along

NOT SO BIG INSIDE OUT

As Julie and I described it in the introduction to this book, our shared vision is that someday all our homes will be designed to integrate interior and exterior, so that they are perceived and lived in as one. When a husband and wife are also architect and landscape architect, there's a wonderful alchemy that takes place, as can be seen in this home—a perfect integration of landscape and building.   —*Sarah*

∧ A Mexican hammock strung between trees offers respite in the garden.

the sometimes-busy street, the whole is enclosed by a 6-ft. wall of concrete, colored pale pink to match the interior walls of the house. The setback and the perimeter wall give privacy and allow Judy's plantings to animate the landscape within. Although the garden was originally designed as a perfect oval grass panel, or lawn, bounded by perennial borders, the planting beds have gradually encroached inward so that, today, the grass panel resembles an asymmetric figure eight. The result is a magnificent interplay between house and garden, geometric and curvilinear forms, and hard and soft surfaces.

Animating the Corners

In a Not So Big House, you're likely to find rooms designed with alcoves or other types of shelter from which to view the main activity of the space. Just like Sarah's principle of shelter around activity, the landscape plan at work here reflects how every square inch is designed for a particular use. With the figure-eight garden occupying the literal and visual center of the yard, each corner takes on a specific role. In the northwest corner

ALL AROUND THE HOUSE

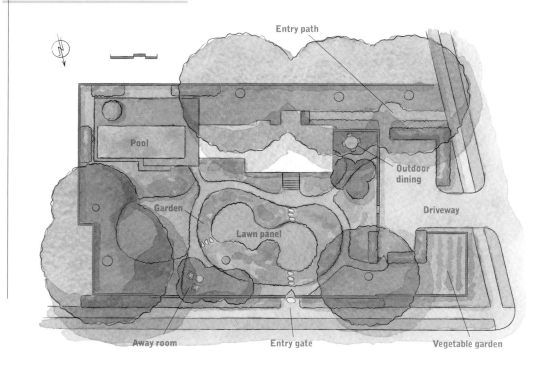

Entry path

Pool

Outdoor dining

Garden

Driveway

Lawn panel

Away room   Entry gate   Vegetable garden

∧ You'd never know that, standing by the vegetable patch, you're just feet away from a busy street corner. Walls and hedges enclose this corner parcel, providing almost complete seclusion.

∧ With so many different places to be—both inside and outside this home—a nearly-empty space provides relief. In this shady corner, the Harmons entertain within the pale pink walls.

< You can place art on outside walls the same way you do inside. A bas-relief panel hangs gracefully on the exterior garden wall.

∧ House and garden are a marriage of opposites: The strict geometry of the floor-to-ceiling glass window walls frames views of the curved beds of the garden.

where two busy streets converge, the Harmons planted a vegetable garden with a plum tree overhanging the wall as an offering to passersby. At the same corner, a Mexican hammock is strung between two trees as an outdoor away room for reading and dozing. And at the southwest quadrant just outside the dining room, a graveled corner of the property is used for entertaining under a canopy of willow oaks, tucked away just yards from the busy street. The Harmon residence is a good example of how, when you

∧ Red, yellow, and blue are considered primary colors because they form the basis for mixtures of other colors. Both red and yellow—like this wall and the metal ladder—are saturated enough to stand up to the bright blue pool.

∨ A Mondrian-like tile design brings together all the colors of the house on the wall by the azure-blue pool.

∧ Divided by an implied walkway, the living room is made up of an intimate, low-ceilinged sitting area around the hearth and a two-story space that fronts on the garden. Looking through a bright red wall, you can see that family room and pool align.

subdivide your property into a series of outdoor rooms with different uses, sizes, shapes, furniture, and plantings, you inhabit the out-of-doors just as you do the different rooms of your house.

Color Inside and Out

In the southeast corner of the property, the couple built a cerulean blue pool as an outdoor extension of the family room. To set off the family-room wing from the pale pink walls of the rest of the house, Frank Harmon painted the outside walls red. In turn, the red becomes part of the decor of the pool garden, a bright space enclosed by low sitting walls that are decorated with vivid mosaic tiles. Potted plants radiate a tropical ambience augmented by black bamboo growing out of a kidney-bean-shaped cutout in the concrete pool deck.

This vibrant house has formed the backdrop for the busy lives of the Harmons, their two children, their clients, and their colleagues, who gather for meetings and social events inside and outside. Set apart and back from the street, the glassy façade of the house opens up to the landscape—an oasis of delight for all who pass through its walls.

< Different tones of the same color can bring harmony to a composition. Here, the gray-blue succulent plant stands out against the light turquoise glazed pot and the deeper hues of the swimming pool.

Enclosing the Whole

When you build a wall around your property, you turn it into one large outdoor living room with four walls, a floor (the lawn and garden), and a ceiling (the high tree canopies overhead and the sky). By framing it, you define and protect what lies inside. And with tall-enough perimeter walls, this enclosure helps to hide your house from view, creating a sense of seclusion. The couple encouraged plants to grow on the 6-ft.-high wall to soften its hard surface and offer a more verdant frontage to their neighbors. By enclosing their site, the Harmons protected their home from the noise of the busy street while extending the presence of home onto their land.

The pale pink stuccoed walls that surround the property are punctuated by a main entryway that lines up with the front door. Two round millstones form the landing.

Low grasses knit the stone steps together as a kind of spillway into the street, softening the hardscape at every turn.

—Julie

outside
parallels

Repeated Form

ARCHITECT FRANK HARMON punctures walls inside and outside his house to great effect. In order to provide a glimpse into the garden from the driveway side of the house, he cut a square opening in the thick perimeter wall. Your eye is drawn to this porthole of light, softened by

the delicate leaves of a clematis vine that peek through. This simple gesture serves to break down the visual barrier between outside and inside while introducing a design theme that he uses in various ways throughout the house.   *—Julie*

Enclosure and Openness

Contrasts heighten our experience of a home. If everything were the same, whether windows and views only in one direction or a single height of ceiling throughout, we wouldn't experience much. But when we add some contrast to the windows and views as the homeowners did here by including long vistas as well as views to places that are more contained, or if we vary the ceiling heights from room to room, then our senses come alive, and we appreciate the qualities of both light and space as a result.

If you look closely at this home, you'll see that inside or out, there is always an elegant interplay of openness and enclosure. Sitting in the living room, for example, you are surrounded by light and windows and view. There's

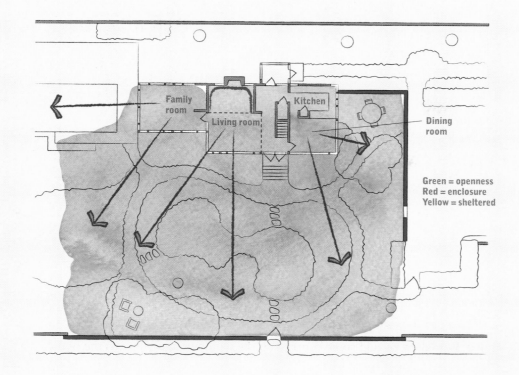

Green = openness
Red = enclosure
Yellow = sheltered

Repeated Form

JUST LIKE outside, inside the house, solid walls define and protect the more private spaces, such as bedrooms, bathrooms, and utility spaces. The opening in the photograph above bears a striking resemblance to the square opening in the surrounding exterior wall (at left). Here again, it is a single puncture in a monolithic surface, giving a glimpse of what lies beyond. Its perfectly square shape is an example of a repeated form. Using a repeated form is one of the easiest architectural tricks for tying inside and outside together, even when the characters of the parts are very different.   —*Sarah*

a real sense of openness. But there is plenty of enclosure as well. The alcove that contains the main seating arrangement is surrounded on three sides by containing walls. Even the ceiling is lower here, giving the space a strong sense of shelter. From this vantage point, it's possible to see a large expanse of garden and sky. The experience is a powerful one because of the contrast between the openness of the view and the enclosure of the alcove.

In the kitchen, enclosure is created by the outside walls—nothing unusual about that. But the openness is far more pronounced than in most rectangular spaces. The windows are a ribbon running the entire length of both walls

and wrapping the corner as well. Seated here, the garden surrounds you like a shawl.

In the bathroom the theme continues. There's enclosure, in this case made by the translucent glass block that allows in light but, appropriately, keeps out view. At the upper part of the wall, where a view presents no privacy problems, the glass block is clear. This is a wonderful example of what I refer to as "view and nonview." Daylight is desirable sometimes even when the view is not.   —*Sarah*

The Harmons decided to locate their house along the south side of the lot in order to give Judy the largest possible area for building a garden. As seen from the outside, the house is composed of two parts: the red-hued family-room wing that abuts the pool and the pale pink main living space—in glass, steel, and concrete—that opens out onto the entry garden.

1	2	3
4	5	6
7	8	9

2 **Simple organic forms** contrast wonderfully with geometric shapes. This kidney-bean-shaped planting bed cut out from the pebble pool deck isolates and accentuates the slender verticality of the black bamboo growing there.

3 6 **Outdoor accessories** bring balance to the garden's palette. The planting tray that rests on the balcony above the front door contains purple plantings that echo the color of the front door and the purple iris nearby.

4 **The oval lawn** appears as a larger version of this little fish pool, since both are bordered by billowing perennials. Allowing plantings to spill over geometric forms and crisp edges makes a space feel inviting and informal, even injecting a sense of romance or mystery that might otherwise not be present.

5 **Hues that are adjacent** on the color wheel—called analogous colors—look harmonious when planted next to each other. Here, yellow yarrow (*Achillea x* 'Moonshine') and sedum flowers match the yellow and green spikes of yucca leaves.

Though a neighbor's home sits just beyond the fence, this house feels secluded, thanks to the cobblestone drive, the native aspen groves, and the entry pond that provides year-round beauty.

A Stream of One's Own

It is rare to discover an available in-town site on the banks of a river and, though local ordinances bar it, very tempting to build a house that faces onto it. The clear challenge of this narrow Aspen, Colorado, site on the Roaring Fork River was to create a unique and functional landscape of home in the space between the property lines while respecting the protective covenants that govern riverfront development here. So landscape architect Suzanne Richman chose to build her own stream.

Suzanne uncovered an existing irrigation ditch and reworked it to become a meandering stream that flows right next to the house. Highlighted with large boulders and small pebbles, flowering perennials, and recirculating water, the stream is punctuated with several pools, each treated as a feature in itself. The resulting woodland rill delights her clients, captures the changing qualities of light

NOT SO BIG INSIDE OUT

Although this home is hardly Not So Big in scale and square footage, the site on which it sits is relatively small. The way the landscape has been crafted to give the impression of a woodland sanctuary is masterful, and it holds many lessons for those of us with smaller dwelling places. The numerous layers of structure, paths, streams, and plantings give the home a sense of both seclusion and expansiveness. It beautifully illustrates how an integrated approach to inside and outside design can give the impression of more territory than there really is. —*Sarah*

∨ Light cast through aspen leaves makes dappled shadows like a pointillist painting across the stream, creating the effect of a natural woodland.

in the reflections on the water, and has truly come to be their landscape of home.

Entering the Realm

At its heart, the landscape of home should be thought of as a realm, a kingdom in the world, and as such, every corner is worthy of thoughtful design. On this property, it's clear from the beginning. Your first view of the striking Arts and Crafts style home comes as you drive down a cobbled lane. Aspen trees narrow the space alongside the drive, and a garden path beckons you under the arched roof of the entry porch. You pass by the first of the water features: a rocky pond occupied by a massive boulder that has been hollowed out to create a basin from which a tiny stream trickles.

On a long, thin site like this, spatial layering, or adding detail at various tiers, helps create a sense of depth along the property line. This third-of-an-acre site has two faces, with the west side speaking to the comfortably scaled east-end Aspen neighborhood and its older homes, and the east side addressing the neighbor's house and

> The posts of the wooden gazebo frame a view of the streambed as it circles around this conical form.

∧ Native cobbles on the driveway provide more than a handsome look; they transport us to a quaint and charming village. The architect chose to hide the garage on the north side of the house.

> Unusual jewellike inserts of glass under the porch rail form a counterpoint to the naturalized plantings along the watercourse.

ALL AROUND THE HOUSE

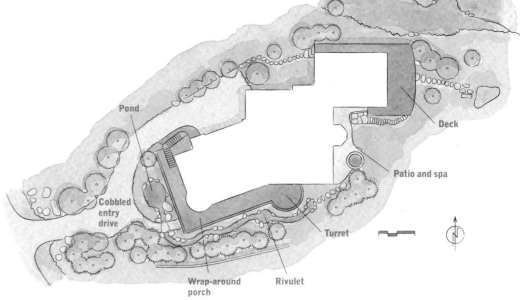

Roaring Fork River

Pond

Deck

Cobbled entry drive

Patio and spa

Turret

N

Wrap-around porch

Rivulet

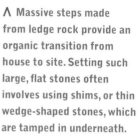

the river with its densely planted slope. At the top of the garden, Suzanne built 6-ft.-high walls and layered in aspen trees to screen the walls so that the close physical boundaries of the site vanish among the vertical layers of leafy vegetation. In front of the aspens, she planted billowing perennials that act as an informal shoreline for a narrow, rocky rivulet.

This little river, a smaller version of the Roaring Fork River, meanders alongside the formal porch with its long sandstone steps into the garden. From a schematic perspective, it's easy to see how these various garden elements add up to a series of parallel lines that move from the built edge of the house outward, becoming ever more natural until they reach the property line. These layers hide and reveal the narrow garden in front of the wall, making it feel more spacious than it actually is.

∧ Skylights cut into the porch roof throw light onto the walking surface in rhythmic patterns. Notice that the same stone that forms the shores of the streambed appears in a foundation wall.

∧ Massive steps made from ledge rock provide an organic transition from house to site. Setting such large, flat stones often involves using shims, or thin wedge-shaped stones, which are tamped in underneath.

< A hot tub occupies another outdoor room, its walls made up of the same pieced stone as the foundation walls. A rounded boulder next to it serves as a pleasing perch.

Creating a Focal Gathering Place

An unusual copper-covered turret room juts out into the garden to form a place to sit, acting as a terminus to both the porch and the streambed. This focal gathering place encourages viewers to step down to the streambed level, where plantings spill over the limestone tread and water. An outdoor away room, this spot frames views of a shady section of the garden and is kept bright by sunlight that pours forth through a small oculus in the roof.

Continuing around the garden, stepping stones take you to an intimate patio with a spa tucked into a stand of aspens and flanked by a round sitting rock. This leads to a large deck and a breakfast nook set in a bay window that overlooks the rushing river. A set of ledgerock steps leads you down to a streamside patio and the shore, where you can glimpse views of the mountainside beyond. Using the strategy of organizing your landscape's design around a nearby natural feature provides one satisfying way to relate your site to its surrounds.

Echoing Nature

The best way to learn how to design an artificial stream is to study how Mother Nature does it. Find a nearby river or brook and take note of how rocks line the shores, where deposit and erosion occur to create bends in the streambed, and how sand and small stones build up to form islands. Be aware of how differently water moves in a deep versus a shallow channel, and notice how many types of waterfalls form along a natural watercourse.

When you are ready to create a brook in your own backyard, don't align your rocks like a string of pearls. Instead, intersperse rocks with patches of moss, ferns, or grasses to break up the stone shoreline; intermingle large boulders with smaller stones; or create small pockets just off the main flow where eddies can occur. By going to the source, you'll end up with a rock grouping, a pond, or a brook that feels like it's always been there.

—Julie

outside

| parallels |

Archetypal Form

ONE OF THE most satisfying ways
to create a seamless landscape design
is to repeat an archetypal form in
different guises. Landscape architect
Suzanne Richman chose a circle,
echoing the geometry used inside the
house. You first encounter the circle
underfoot, as you walk across a metal

grate that hides the mechanical system
of the stream.

In the railings that protect the porch,
jewellike spheres of glass dazzle the
eye as light plays across them. In the
away-room turret, the roof is circular,
and the oculus—a circular opening—
washes light across the interior copper
shingles. These small but significant
repeating forms act like signposts that
carry you through the property and
into the house.   *—Julie*

HOMESCAPING

Layering

Julie has described how layers of plant material,
such as aspen trees, have been used around
the edges of the property to create a secluded
environment. But if you look closely, you'll discover
that the same principle of layering has been applied throughout the design
to create a gradation of interior to exterior places. One of the most obvious of
these layers is the wraparound porch, which creates a covered outdoor realm
in which to sit or stroll. Although it is outdoor space, it is a part of the house.
Does that mean it is landscaping or architecture? It's both.

A seat in the living room provides a view through large windows defined by a distinctive pattern of muntins (the small dividers in each window). The pattern establishes the windows as a layer of see-through structure. And beyond this is the outdoor realm of the porch covered by the wide eaves above. The vegetation beyond this is the final layer in the gradient from inside to out.

The benefit of creating such layers is that while one space is only partially obscured from the next, each is clearly defined by its respective material, whether that be muntins, eaves, or plantings. Just as punctuation is used in a sentence to make it more comprehensible, layering allows your eyes to understand more easily what they are looking at, and it creates the perception that there is more to see. If you were to remove the muntins, lop off the eaves and porch, and remove the stream and the aspens, the property would actually seem much smaller and a lot less engaging.

—Sarah

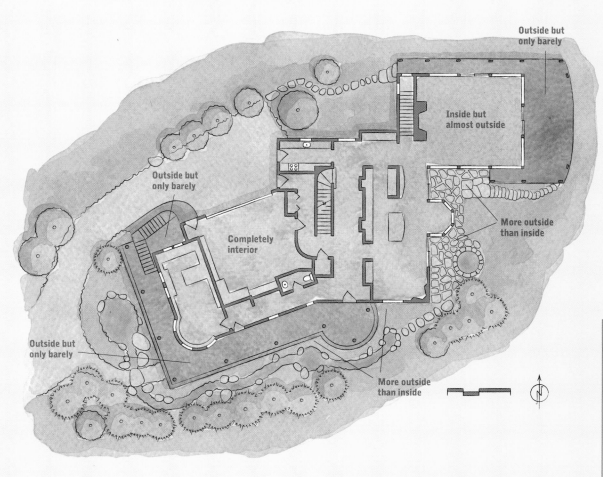

Outside but only barely

Inside but almost outside

Outside but only barely

Completely interior

More outside than inside

Outside but only barely

More outside than inside

Archetypal Form

THE EYEBROW window that plays a dominant role from the outside has an equally essential role on the interior. After parking in the garage, the homeowners are welcomed inside by this view, giving them a glimpse of the living space. The wing wall seen to the left of the opening obscures the kitchen but allows the eye to take in the complete form of the eyebrow.

When you are using an archetypal form, it's not always necessary to use the entire form to establish a sense of connection to other parts of the house. Whereas outside the complete circle is used, inside the form is subtle, as in the eyebrow and in the second-floor balcony.

—Sarah

A curving wall embraces this house and garden, setting them apart from a parched desert setting. Conceiving of the home and garden as one reality, the architect and landscape architect created an oasis of beauty and serenity.

Shelter and Embrace

When visitors first spot this Santa Fe, New Mexico, residence, it looks like a classic adobe structure in a neighborhood of similar homes baking in the brilliant desert sun. By ordinance, much of the area around the house was relandscaped to match the juniper savanna ecosystem that surrounds the site, asserting the natural dominance of the desert with its low rainfall, exposed and windy setting, and low-humus soils. But move closer to the house, and the differences between this property and those around it become apparent. The "choreography" of the entrance, or the sequence that visitors are meant to follow—the portals that protect, the walls that embrace, the interplay of light and shade, and the beauty of the setting—all contribute to what makes this a special place.

NOT SO BIG INSIDE OUT

In very flat country, many houses look as though they've landed on their sites from outer space because there's little or no integration between house and site. This New Mexico home is, by contrast, beautifully integrated into the land, despite the challenges presented by its location. Julie and I love its connection to the terrain, as well as its sophisticated development of exterior and interior living places.   —Sarah

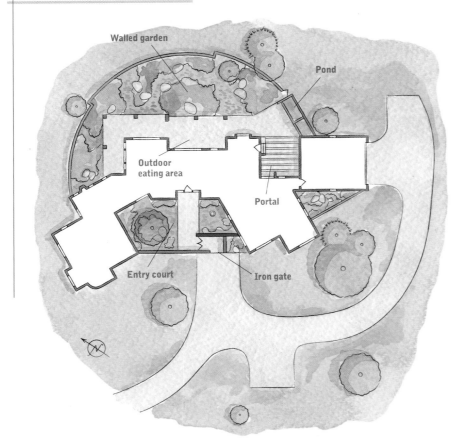

Walled garden

Pond

Outdoor eating area

Portal

Entry court

Iron gate

∧ The low-slung house, reminiscent of a traditional adobe, seems to grow right out of the desert landscape. The swooping curve of the driveway reminds us of the curved garden wall that embraces this home.

∧ Thick walls stand up to the harsh conditions. Once inside the iron gates, visitors are greeted by a landscaped courtyard that offers a more benign setting.

Move inside the walls of this residence, and you begin to experience space as it unfolds in layers. From the guest parking area, a pair of freestanding stucco walls reminiscent of traditional adobe beckons. Like two arms reaching out, the walls are offset from each other, creating an entry portal, a feature typical to southwestern architecture, two steps up from grade. Full-height openwork iron gates lead to an inner courtyard where a surprising thing happens: What had been adobe-colored walls on the outside are a deep and satisfying red stucco on the inside. This entry courtyard is spare and open, with a single Russian olive tree, a few clumps of ornamental grasses, and a sculpture of a cactus. A wide path bisects the space, leading directly through a full-size door on pivots into the center of the house. From here, there is a view through the house and into a walled garden full of flowering perennials.

< The front door pivots inward to reveal a view clear through the house out to the garden and beyond. The unadorned opening is a solid version of the almost-frameless windows that adjoin it.

∧ Color has been subtly modulated in the entry courtyard. The rusty hues of a cactus sculpture are picked up in the far wall and contrast with the near wall, a deep vermilion.

Portals that Protect

With its dramatic views to the surrounding mountain ranges, the native landscape is breathtaking. Here, outdoor living can be enjoyed throughout most of the year, especially when protected from the high-altitude sun and southwesterly winds. One way that the designers chose to set off the distant views from within the house was to use a porchlike transitional area between house and garden. This portal replaces traditional wooden porch posts with modern pillars clad in stucco. Their depth, combined with the heavy roof, shades the generous sliding glass doors. The portals help bring nature into the house and draw people into the garden.

∨ Good design often depends upon the deft use of transitional spaces, offering protection from the elements and opening to significant views and the intimate landscape. Here, a wide masonry post supports a deep beam to form the portal.

∧ Where the portal ends, the geometry of the terrace changes, creating a transitional path to the pond by the kitchen patio. The square frame of the window acts like a porthole in a ship, focusing the view from within while reflecting the sky.

Embracing Walls

A curved courtyard wall gracefully encloses the garden on the northeast side of the house, creating a private space that harkens back to the architectural traditions of the Southwest. Inside, a brilliantly colored xeriscape—a landscape of plantings that need little water in order to survive—includes bold combinations of perennials and ornamental grasses arranged in naturalized drifts, with the occasional river-washed boulder placed as an accent in the rock mulch. Splashes of color, including the yellow black-eyed Susans and the mustard-colored walls, play off against the complementary lavender hues of the Russian sage.

The same light purple colors the outer wall by the kitchen, a mediating shade between water and sky. Water pours out from a metal channel into a long rectangular trough; the sounds and sight of the silvery liquid add a sensory accent to the outdoor eating area under the wooden pergola.

Solid and Translucent

In the desert, solid walls surround a house to keep harsh light, wind, heat, and cold from penetrating within; they are punctured only when special sensory effects are desired. Here, the architect played the thickness of walls against the transparency of glass. The thick rim of stucco that borders the square kitchen window, for instance, turns the see-through glass into a framed picture. Seen from the outside, the picture becomes a mirror of walls and sky; from the inside, the glass becomes invisible, bringing the sunlit garden right into the dark, cool kitchen. Dramatic night lighting turns the house into a lantern, the interior contrasting effectively with the solidity of the building's walls and portals. In this harsh environment, the landscape of home thrives best within the shelter of embracing walls.

THE LANDSCAPE OF HOME

Oasis in the Desert

In dry landscapes, the appearance of water can feel like a miracle. Here, this silvery elixir of life falls from the mouth of a simple metal scupper, its source unknown. This little rectangular pond turns this garden into an oasis—literally, a fertile ground in the desert where the existence of water allows plants to grow and travelers to replenish water supplies. For the homeowners, it brings visual, sensory, and thermal delight, with the lavender-blue walls adding a sense of calm.

Bringing water into our backyard landscapes always stimulates and soothes. We are captivated by the reflections of clouds on a still reflecting pool and mesmerized by the ripples of a bubbler. Jets enthrall by the upward thrust of their sprays, and waterfalls fascinate as they cascade into a waiting pool. Even the simplest birdbath offers hours of enjoyment, as birds chirp and flitter, enlivening our landscapes and our enjoyment of them.

—Julie

Light Intensity Variation

A PLACE with intensely bright sunlight shows us how to use the contrast between light and shade to bring an extra dimension to our landscapes. On clear days, you can find four different light conditions in the garden. Unobstructed sunlight highlights and defines forms, such as this white rock.

Deep shadows caused by obstructions such as buildings, walls, or trees

provide thermal relief in desert climates. Broken light is the pattern of sunlight and shade created by light passing through objects such as latticework, trellises, or tree branches. Here, openwork beams cast diagonal stripes across an outdoor eating area. Dappled light through trees makes patches of light.   *—Julie*

HOMESCAPING

Almost-Frameless Windows and Doors

One of my favorite techniques for blurring the boundary between inside and outside is to employ a technique that I call "almost-frameless windows and doors." By minimizing the frame of an opening in a wall, ideally stretching it all the way to each of the adjacent surfaces—the floor, the ceiling, and the sidewalls—our eyes are led to believe that there really is no window there at all.

In this home, you can readily see just how effective the technique is. Because the windows and door fill each opening, it appears that the space flows out into the courtyard beyond, unobstructed. The ribbonlike black frames all but disappear, making the inside and outside spaces seem like parts of a single whole.

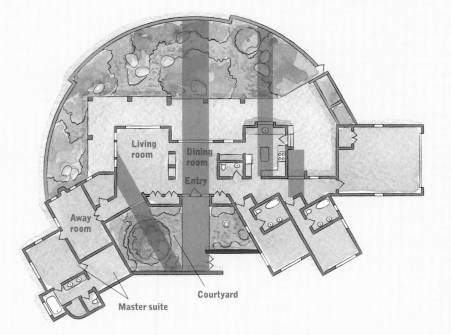

Light Intensity Variation

A HOUSE that lets in a lot of sunlight in a hot climate can be extremely uncomfortable. But here, the architect has allowed only occasional brilliance amid a more measured approach to letting in the natural light. Notice the difference in light quality between the brightness of the bookshelves, lit from skylights above; the brilliant light entering through the small, unprotected square windows at the top of the room; and the more subtle daylight provided by the sliding door, protected from direct sunlight by the overhang above. There's even daylight reflected on the ceiling coming in from the glass door. In combination, these sources give a wide range of light intensities that make the space a delight to experience. *—Sarah*

Another place you can use this effect is at kitchen countertops. By bringing the window all the way down to the countertop surface, so there's no back-splash, and by extending the side window all the way to the adjacent perpendicular wall surface, the window itself is played down, while the connection to the outside is played up. Once again, there is the illusion that you are completely connected with the exterior surroundings. Add even a small backsplash, however, and the experience disappears. It's the unobstructed flow of space that makes it work.

—Sarah

The way we perceive color is affected by many factors: time of day, latitude, altitude, season, and cultural conditioning, to name just a few (night lighting is an art in itself). Here, warm interior lighting filters through the glass sliders into the portals, where ceiling fixtures add a soft glow in the twilight.

1	2	3
4	5	6
7	8	9

4 **In sunny climates,** it pays to use vivid colors in the landscape, since bright light tends to wash color out. From the cool shade cast by the broken light across the teak table and chairs, the lavender wall seems to match the sky.

5 **Sandwiched between** the earth-tone garden wall and the muted interior, the brilliant purple Russian sage focuses the eye on the middle distance.

6 **9** **Notice how,** in full sun, bright colors fade out but the detail of dark greens pops out. In full shade the opposite is true: Bright colors tend to stand out, and dark colors lose their detail.

9 **Ornamental grasses** combine with just a few hardy perennials—Russian sage (*Perovskia atriplicifolia*) and black-eyed Susans (*Rudbeckia fulgida*)—to vivid effect.

Flow

Composing Journeys

Flow

Journeys around your property

include ways to enter, exit,

pause, stop, and view

in a continuous flow.

A threshold of cut bluestone pavers offers a pausing place along the stepping-stone path, where a gateway is adorned by clematis vines. The large, diamond-shaped stone signals this temporary stopping point.

Variations on a Theme

The Fox residence is a tiny, seemingly modest property that is full of magic. People who visit this Berkeley, California, home are drawn from the unassuming front yard down a path along a side yard and into a secret garden in the back. Landscape architect Charles McCulloch choreographed the design of the property of his clients, Berkeley architect Dennis Fox and his gardener wife, Mary. Using one material—bluestone—in a variety of shapes, sizes, and finishes, McCulloch organized an elegant journey from street to backyard, with many horticultural pleasures and other special "events" along the way.

The neat front yard with its slate walk, lawn, and foundation plantings offers few clues about what lies beyond the gray stucco walls. The first surprise is that where one might expect to find the side driveway, a garden has been made. Here, stone is the theme.

NOT SO BIG INSIDE OUT

Just because you have a small house and an equally small yard, it doesn't mean that you can't make a very beautiful and secluded haven. As you'll see in this California home, every space both inside and out has been designed to make the entire composition a delight. Woven together with an underlying geometrical order, it beautifully illustrates how the application of a few simple tricks can transform "too small" into "just right."
— *Sarah*

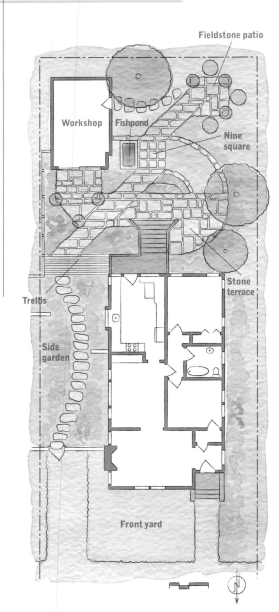

Fieldstone patio

Workshop

Fishpond

Nine square

Trellis

Side garden

Stone terrace

Front yard

> **Flat fieldstones wander their way through this side garden—an elegant replacement for a former driveway.**

Λ The sloping backyard of the Foxes' house has been terraced into three levels. The sophisticated path system moves visitors through the spaces to a terrace built for two at the bottom of the garden.

< A long gateway stretches from the railing of the upper deck across the entry to the backyard, forming an arbor that is covered in clematis and rose vines. The latticework on the deck continues as low fencing by the gate, allowing a glimpse through.

Low stone walls separate landscape from street, and flat fieldstone stepping stones meander their way through the plantings where the driveway once was. Tall trees give privacy and intensify the experience of the path by narrowing down the width and lengthening the spatial experience.

A Gateway at Home

At the back corner of the house, a framed opening extends the wall of the house into the landscape, beckoning you to walk through to the secret garden beyond. But even as you are drawn to this clematis-covered gateway, a cut-stone threshold, what I call a "pausing place," makes you stop a moment before moving on (see the photo on p. 68). A square of bluestone, rotated so it looks like a diamond, occupies the middle of a small terrace of oblong stones, making it feel like a welcome mat. Here, we are introduced to a shape that will dominate the pathways in the Foxes' backyard garden. The diamonds continue as stepping stones along a diagonal axis into the backyard.

Laying Down a Grid

As he planned the garden, Charles McCulloch divided the backyard schematically into nine large squares, then drew a diagonal pathway across this implied grid to create a long line of sight. He arranged distinctly different landscape elements within the three rows created by the grid (see p. 74). By the house, he designed a stone terrace that overlooks the garden, which acts as one of several destination points from which the garden can be viewed. Charles designed the second row of the grid as a panel or section

V Looking at the front yard of the Foxes' house, you would never know that beyond it lies a flowery paradise.

of grass terminating in a fishpond. The lowest terrace—the last section of the grid—sits at the back property line and is planted with various woodland plant species to screen the neighbors and add privacy. A small fieldstone patio nestles into the plantings, offering intimate seating and views back up the slope toward the house and garden. Combining this nine-square grid and the diagonal path is a master stroke that makes the tiny space feel larger by subtly organizing the space into parts that are linked by the strong linear journey through them.

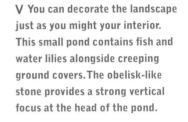

∨ You can decorate the landscape just as you might your interior. This small pond contains fish and water lilies alongside creeping ground covers. The obelisk-like stone provides a strong vertical focus at the head of the pond.

< A pad made up of nine concrete squares acts as a terrace as well as an orienting device in this backyard landscape.

∧ Collections can form the backbone of your garden. Homeowner Mary Fox, a talented gardener, loves succulent plants. At the edge of the stone terrace, her collection spills out of planting areas built into the wall.

Knuckles in the Landscape

What designers refer to as a "knuckle" is the place where things come together in a space: nodal points or pivot points where special events happen. Here, these knuckles occur at the intersections of the grid lines and the diagonal path. Plants, pavements, and the small pond were all placed within the grid or at significant intersections of grid lines and the diagonal path. The most obvious knuckle that draws the eye and gives order to the whole composition is the nine squares of paving that rest in the very middle of the garden space. These paving squares stand for the implied grid, which viewers never see, but intuit as an organizing device in this elegant landscape. The large square pavers are parallel to the woodshed and the house, and they move the visitor through the site and over to the far corner of the garden. Designing a knuckle that interconnects all the parts at once can be the trickiest part of a landscape to design, but it's also the most satisfying. It's like fitting the last piece of the jigsaw puzzle into place; the whole design suddenly pulls into focus.

Intimate Immensity

Playing with the scale of the features in your landscape gives added visual interest. I find that objects that are tiny or huge in relation to me tend to hold my attention longer than something scaled to my size. Part of this enchantment lies in a paradox: When I look at the presidential faces on Mount Rushmore, am I petite or huge in relation to them? My body is much smaller, but my mind is immense as it rushes to examine President Roosevelt's face close up. When it comes to understanding scale, imagination may be more compelling than reality.

At the Fox residence, the small pool with its standing stones next to a fairy statue acts as a miniature landscape next to the nine overscaled paving stones. The owners planted these focal points with small-leafed perennials and placed miniature water lilies in the pool to preserve the sense of an intimate scale in this already tiny garden. On the terrace, Mary Fox, the gardener in the family, planted a collection of her favorite sedums, which add a delicate size and texture to a relatively large expanse of pavers.

—Julie

outside
| parallels |

Pattern and Geometry

USING REPEATING patterns in a landscape helps make it intelligible to a viewer. The nine-square pattern that forms the focal point focuses your attention and organizes the space into components. The ironwork pattern of the stair railing—three rails and a space—is repeated in the rails of the fence at the back. As you look at the photo, notice how your eye follows the

pattern of dark verticals spaced in threes around the garden.

Mary Fox also uses container plantings on the stairs in a repeating pattern. These use the same textures and colors found in her sedum collection on the terrace. Using pattern to reveal underlying design themes brings a level of sophistication and coherence to your landscape. —*Julie*

Organizing Strategy

In discussing the layout of the garden, Julie describes an imaginary grid over the entire backyard to give an underlying order—what I call an "organizing strategy"—to the design. Organizing strategies, while not always obvious to a home's inhabitants, can help give it a sense of balance and meaning.

The basic organizing strategy for this house is a simple rectangle, covered by an equally simple hipped roof with a front gable. Looking at the floor plan, you can see that there are no extra corners, bump-outs, or cantilevers, which would have added to the construction cost.

But just because it's simple in form doesn't mean it has to be boring. Often these constraints provide the catalysts for creativity. While in the back garden the nine-square pattern provides a point of focus, on the interior, the informal eating area is the focal gathering place. If you look closely again at the plan above, you'll see that the eating area is almost exactly at the center of the property. It's one of the most comfortable places to sit, and its placement, at the center of the land and at the boundary between inside and out, makes it feel like the most important and connected place in the house.

Point of focus on 9 square terrace

Point of focus on kitchen table

Site centerline

Site centerline

The eating-area window is aligned with the outdoor stairway leading down into the garden, which in turn is roughly aligned with the nine squares, so as you move through the house, from living room to dining room to kitchen, there's a strong axis, and a long view through the house, that's aligned with the pathway into the garden. Alignments like this can give a subliminal but powerful sense of order to a home.

The original house had double-hung windows with a six-over-six-pane and four-over-four-pane pattern, but in the remodel, architect Dennis Fox used casement windows with a four-pane pattern. He brought the windowsills all the way down to countertop height so that someone standing in the kitchen has more connection to the garden.　　*—Sarah*

Pattern and Geometry

WHILE OUTSIDE the house, the geometric pattern of nine square pavers attracts our attention; inside, the application of pattern is less noticeable. Yet the role it plays is very much the same. This home, like many older homes, has windows with dividers, or muntins, to break up the view. The muntins are a simple pattern overlaying the window. They give us something to look at in addition to seeing what's beyond. Although in modern houses this is less common, many homeowners enjoy the feeling of intimacy that muntins give to the interior. Smaller segments of anything create a more approachable scale. If they were to be removed, the house would lose its cozy feel.　　*—Sarah*

This **Not So Big House** on a small lot is packed with opportunities to learn about good design. Inside and out, landscape and architecture are brought into harmony along the home's carefully crafted paths and places.

1	2	3
4	5	6
7	8	9

3 **This flower vase,** filled with roses from the garden, embellishes the corner window in the kitchen. Wherever you look, blooms bring the outside in.

1 **Homeowner Mary Fox's** nosegays adorn different areas of the house, including a niche in the bathroom.

9 **Mary's collection** of succulents is augmented by many species, including the genus *Sedum*, *Sempervivum*, and *Crassula*. The owners left small planting pockets in the stone steps leading to the middle terrace.

6 **An Australian** plant called "Kangaroo paw" (*Anigozanthos* "Bush gold") adds a vivid hue as well as texture to a garden palette.

Two stones occupy a circular "pool" of gravel in my clients' front yard.
Every inch of the raised ranch and its environs has been altered and
improved.

Japanese Journey

Drive past this renovated raised ranch in a Boston suburb, and you just may have to pull over and gape. The front yard has been turned into an otherworldly landscape—a verdant terraced garden centered around a circular "pool" of gravel. Two stones—one standing, another "floating" upon the gravel's surface—focus the eye. I designed this garden for the homeowners, who, to my good fortune, had a strong artistic bent. The garden forms the beginning of a landscape journey that encircles the house from front to back and feels like a geometric version of a Japanese garden.

Redesigned by architect Linda Hamlin, the house is now a glassy, open structure that allows views from the front yard through to the back. Double doors and casement windows open out to the front garden; floor-to-ceiling sliders extend the living room out onto the

NOT SO BIG INSIDE OUT

This ordinary ranch house has been transformed into an evocative metaphorical landscape in which the views from inside, as well as the paths and places contained by the home's surroundings, connote a journey of wonder and delight. With gravel symbolizing water, stepping stones for islands, and a teahouse standing in for a foreign land, there's exploration and discovery possible with every glance and in every step.
—*Sarah*

back deck, obscuring the distinction between inside and out. Sitting above the street, the house lights up like a lantern at night.

Geometric Japanese
At its most basic, the landscape outside a house should be like this one—a series of paths and places that owners can choreograph as a journey through space. Here, the garden journey is made up of a simple palette of bluestone squares and oblongs that travel over gravel, grass, and plantings to end up at a little teahouse on a hill in the backyard. While Japanese in spirit, the garden is designed using distinctly un-Japanese forms: circles, squares, and S-curves.

A path of cut bluestone takes you around the side of the house to the backyard, where large perimeter trees and an upward-facing slope create a bowllike feeling from the ground. To organize this space, I used a traditional Japanese technique called *karesansui* or "dry mountain river" style. Such gardens feel like an abstracted—and dry—version of a natural landscape, often including miniature hills, islands, and watercourses without water represented by raked patterns in gravel or sand. With this technique in mind, I created a large circular "pond" made up of chunks of gravel and placed a

∧ "Mouse-hole" entries like this low gateway increase the sense of anticipation about what's ahead on the landscape. Here, a pruned beech leads to a Japanese teahouse.

< Inside and outside converge at the living-room sliders that lead directly onto a wooden deck. An openwork trellis structure overhead is covered with vines in summer, adding a "ceiling" to this outdoor room.

∨ The owners altered every surface in the front yard, including their driveway, where they used square concrete pavers. Against this, a concrete retaining wall is softened with billowing Japanese juniper.

Pools of Space

In keeping with the idea of creating a geometric Japanese-style garden, I designed a circular "pond" of gravel in the front yard and placed in it two large granite boulder "islands" hand-selected from a local quarry. Echoing the species, texture, and color of the white pines that edged the property, I brought in dwarf pines and Japanese juniper, making an abstract evergreen shoreline surrounding the pond.

Designing the open space of a landscape as a pool—whether of actual water or gravel, sand, or even plantings or turf—allows you to create a pleasing form in an otherwise amorphous landscape. A pool needs a clean edge for the shoreline, so it's important to use different materials, such as steel or wood on end, or create a line of cobbles, brick, or stone. The best way to make your pool look natural is to use different-size stones and leave spaces for plantings, just as Mother Nature does. Also, I shy away from using plastic or other manmade materials as edgings, because they tend not to lose their sheen or develop a natural patina.

—Julie

< I organized the landscape as a journey from front to back, in to out, down to up, and closed to open. Here, the deck's stair railings lead eye and foot directly into the garden.

square of grass that seems to float like an island over the "watery" landscape.

Used at the time by the homeowner's young son as a play space, the square of grass lies at a 45-degree angle to the house. Its diagonal placement brings energy into the otherwise circular design of the backyard. On a slope at the upper corner of the garden, a wooden teahouse looks back onto the house, set almost perfectly parallel to the diagonal lawn. It is, of course, the destination point of this garden journey. Along the way, a path of thick bluestone stepping-stones takes visitors on a journey around the garden, with smaller squares designed for one step each and large squares set as pausing places. Here, there's room to plant both feet and let your eyes

∧ Using cut bluestone squares and oblongs of different sizes as path material, I linked the whole together as a design of stepping stones and raised stone "bridges," as pleasing to look at as it is to walk along.

∧ The lovely perennial known by its less lovely common name, Toad lily, accentuates the elegant structure of the garden.

< The teahouse peeks out over a hillside of mountain laurel, its diagonal placement chosen to give the longest view across the garden. Placed on a 45-degree angle to the house, it lines up with the square of grass.

> A "watercourse" cascades down the hill from under the teahouse to culminate in swaths of washed pea gravel, grass, mulch, and gray river stone just past low-growing bamboo that edges the "shoreline."

ALL AROUND THE HOUSE

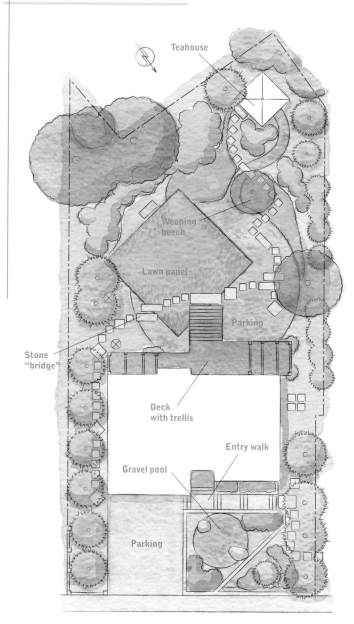

Teahouse

Weeping beech

Lawn panel

Parking

Stone "bridge"

Deck with trellis

Entry walk

Gravel pool

Parking

wander upward and into the garden. I also raised long slabs of bluestone up on foundations as "bridges" that allow a slightly higher vantage onto the garden.

Stepping-stones move through "water" and "shoreline," ducking under a gateway formed by the bough of a weeping beech tree, and finally wind their way up the hillside to the teahouse above. A "stream" of gravel pours down from under the teahouse to the pond in an elegant S-curve. At the top of the hill, you can finally stop and take stock of where you've been, retracing the path of your allegorical voyage through time and space. It helps to think of your landscape as a spatial journey through your property, linking different events along a continuously changing path. When you voyage forth into the nature of your own backyard, it's likely you will find yourself somewhere along the way.

outside
parallels

Framed Openings

IN THE NATURAL landscape, you can find framed openings everywhere. Tree trunks act like upright borders, or a break in a hedge line serves as gateway. At this property I designed, framed openings abound. For example, the teahouse at the top of the hill is

structured so that one person or an intimate twosome can look out at the garden. A built-in bench nestles next to an alcove in a stucco wall. Wooden posts do double duty, supporting the roof structure as well as framing the views to the landscape below. Set into the sidewall, a circular window and two triangular clerestories bring the forest into the small building.

—Julie

Openability

Although in this country we like to use the occasional sliding door to connect us to our surroundings, it's rare that we will use multiple sliding units "ganged" together, as in this home. The effect, when done well, is to minimize the boundary between inside and out and to allow passage to the out-of-doors wherever your

heart desires. With the long platform deck that extends across its entire back face, the whole house feels like a screened porch—you're almost outside, no matter where you are. When the surroundings are beautiful, this can make the house seem much more engaging. You are borrowing the character of the outside to provide animated and colorful "wallpaper" for the home's interior.

If you are familiar with traditional Japanese architecture, you'll know that translucent shoji screens and solid sliding screens called *amado* substitute for solid exterior walls, so there's always a strong interconnection between inner and outer worlds. When the boundary is movable, it's easier to see that both in and out are states of mind as much as they are locations. When interior and exterior are woven together as one in a home, the experience of the interior world feeds that of the outer world, and vice versa. I often think of interior space as simply a sheltered position from which to experience the outer world.

—Sarah

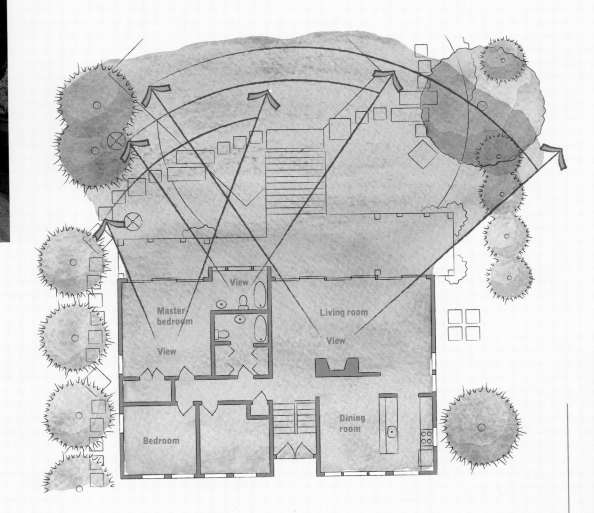

Framed Openings

A WIDE DOORWAY or archway is a lot like a picture frame. With doors wide open, it literally frames the view beyond, drawing attention to it and making it a sort of canvas. It takes a designer's eye to recognize and work with a framed view, as Julie has here.

Notice that although the gravel "pool" is not centered on the framed opening, the boulder is. It becomes the point of focus from the front entryway out to the street. Imagine how much less inviting this view would be if there were only a front lawn beyond the retaining wall and the steps. There would be nothing to draw your attention outward, and the retaining wall itself would become the focus.

—Sarah

This home is a study in the differentiation of materials and elements. For example, the downspout, a special and separate form, becomes a surprising point of focus on the façade.

Parallel Paths

Architect George Suyama's dream was to design a house on his narrow beachfront property located in an old summer getaway community on the Puget Sound in Washington. On the site there existed two structures: a bunkhouse and a one-bedroom log cabin, which sit just steps from the beach. Designed to respect the fragile nature of the site, the minimalist house George built perches back up the hillside, standing in stark contrast to the older rustic cottages.

Built on a sliver of a lot, the house follows the grade from a high point at street level, moving down a full story as it makes its way toward the sound. The house is designed as two parallel journeys: one for people, the other for water. Entering the house from the street, visitors pass through a series of cast-concrete walls as they walk along a floor of polished concrete. To the right lies a

NOT SO BIG INSIDE OUT

What struck Julie and me about this home is the amazing integration of indoor and outdoor spaces. So blended are they that the terms don't seem to make much sense here—a remarkable achievement on so small a piece of land with so small a house. Landscape and building are components in a singular sculpture for living in. It's truly a remarkable illustration of what *katei*, the all-encompassing Japanese term for "house and garden," can really mean.   —*Sarah*

> A watercourse brings movement into an otherwise static space. Hidden from the street by a cast-concrete wall, a channel is fed by a small weir—a dam that holds the source of the water.

∧ From the street, it's clear just how narrow waterfront properties can be. The house, buried behind the garage, is hidden from view.

watercourse that flows as a series of stepped terraces alongside the house. It begins as a small reservoir by the front door, turns into a long narrow canal that runs under a cantilevered wooden deck, and disappears for a time until it reemerges at the lower level of the house.

Unadorned Details

On the left, along the implied corridor, lies a series of rooms—indoor and outdoor—that are protected by one long roof structure. The first is an outdoor living room centered

< Two cottages face the water while the Suyamas' new house gazes out from above.

on a hearth, providing warmth and visual delight to an otherwise austere space under a ceiling of open roof joists. You begin to read a particular design ethic in the crafting of each material, each connection, each detail. Walls are unadorned, posts rise from the simplest of bases, rafter tails are sawn straight, unchamfered.

Stroll and Mind Journeys

What I term a "stroll journey" is a physical voyage you take on foot around a landscape; a "mind journey" is the mental voyage that occurs when your body is at rest and your mind is engaged by a scene, view, or focal point. Both journeys occur at the Suyamas' house. You take a stroll journey as you move past glass walls into the heated living area, entering the combined kitchen and dining room. The long, narrow nature of this space is emphasized by a series of lines: A bank of cabinets runs the length of the south wall, lit by a long, narrow window set over the sink. Across from the dining table that stretches down the middle of the room, a band of high windows encourages views of the tree canopy along the side of the property. As you

Λ The wall signals a change in level for foot traffic and the water that falls from a metal chute. The first of many oblong shapes— this time an opening in the wall—is cut into the concrete.

> Elegant spaces are created from the simplest of details. Here, it appears that long blocks of wood were laid on end across the channel wall to create a cantilevered deck.

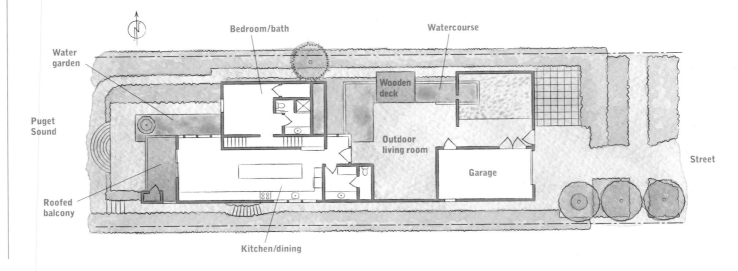

Labels on plan: Water garden · Bedroom/bath · Watercourse · Wooden deck · Puget Sound · Outdoor living room · Street · Roofed balcony · Garage · Kitchen/dining

∨ This plant seems to dance in its pot, bringing a sense of movement and playfulness to the handsome vessel in which it is planted.

∧ Vertical shapes demand our attention, whereas long, horizontal shapes feel restful to the eye. Oblongs abound in the furniture, cabinetry, and decor of the entry terrace.

move to the end of the room, toward the light and views of the sound, you leave the interior space to stand on a roofed balcony. You've reached a destination point of the stroll journey, what I call the "mind journey." Here your body is in repose while your mind is engaged with movement on the water, enjoying views of ferries, fishing vessels, and distant islands.

The journeys continue as you venture down a flight of stairs to the private realm of master bedroom and bath. Here, the watercourse reemerges as a sluiceway that cuts through a thick wall, pouring into a perimeter pool that borders two sides of the

∧ Water and light interweave in the master bath, half a floor below the street level. Tracks in the floor, wall, and ceiling allow glass doors to roll shut, providing shelter from the elements.

∧ Look through this concrete slot, and you will see the metal sluiceway that bridges entry pond and bathroom pool. A smooth stone sits just above the mouth, dividing the water enough to create patterns as it streams.

∨ A water garden forms the terminus for the watery journey. Here, floating leaf aquatics, like the water lilies pictured here (*Nymphaea spp.*) and lotus (*Nelumbo spp.*) usually have roots at a depth of 1 ft. to 3 ft. below the surface of the water.

∧ A basement window opens out to the water garden, reflecting the bamboo, ferns, and iris planted to soften the perimeter fence. The windows, walls, fences, and vegetation are carefully placed, making the narrow lot seem much more expansive.

bathroom. Once again, the boundaries between inside and outside almost completely disappear. Open to the sky, the narrow watercourse can be closed off by floor-to-ceiling glass sliders. As it moves through the bedroom, the watercourse again disappears, surfacing outside the walls of the house as a water garden before it circulates back to the start of the journey once more. This simple yet elegant home is crafted with an astonishing level of care. Outside dissolves into inside; stroll journeys parallel mind journeys; the whole is a habitable work of art.

Animating Influences

Architect George Suyama's house is a study in careful control; everything seems exactly right. Yet in the deepest, most inward-looking place—the wine cellar in the basement—a surprise awaits: a pair of old glassy French doors, elements that are clearly not of George's fashioning. Japanese masters speak of creating something imperfect within the perfection of their gardens; these gates speak to memory and the surprise of the accidental in this otherwise immaculate environment. Their patina also recalls the beginning of the journey: the rustic cabins perched at water's edge, which predate the house itself.

Upstairs, in the kitchen/dining room, another surprise awaits the visitor, an element quite different from the otherwise perfect order and control. An antlerlike branch sprawls over the long dining table, its curves and rough edges disturbing the geometric perfection of the room. Without it, the room might feel too serious, self-conscious, even staid. Instead, it lives and breathes. The "accident" enlivens the whole.   —Julie

outside
p a r a l l e l s

Differentiation of Parts

ARCHITECT GEORGE SUYAMA crafted his home by clearly differentiating its parts. Each building element—wall, beam, sluiceway, roof edge—is made of a different material and treated separately. For example, where the gravel drip space abuts the wooden border of the flat roof (below), it lies separated by a metal edge.

Plantings here work in the same way. Bamboos, ground covers, and water plants are massed separately so you can see the color, texture, and form of each type of plant.   *—Julie*

Blurring the Boundary

The aspect of this house that delights me the most is the ambiguousness of what's outside and what's inside. In previous chapters, I describe how almost-frameless windows can help to minimize the separation between interior and exterior, but this house takes this concept to a new level. For example, at this entry door, the wall all but disappears. It's made entirely of glass with the most minimal of frames abutting the rafters above. This transparency stands in stark contrast to the solidity of the adjacent stucco wall, which continues into the house on the other side of the door. In the same way, the sturdy beam supporting the roof structure above the courtyard continues

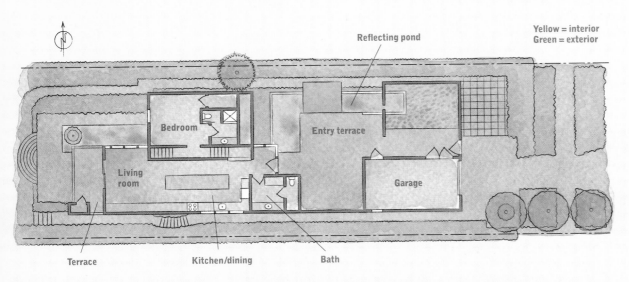

Yellow = interior
Green = exterior

Reflecting pond

Bedroom

Entry terrace

Living room

Garage

Terrace

Kitchen/dining

Bath

Differentiation of Parts

THE CONCEPT of differentiation of parts in design is analogous to the type of fine cooking where each ingredient is separately prepared and displayed on the plate. Each element is strongly stated, but connected by placement rather than intermingling. The platform (below) is a separate plane, accessed by a separate folded black metal plate, a stairway. Even the railing is pulled away from the steps to differentiate it as a separate object.

Now look at the objects on the center table, and you'll see the same attitude applied to the accessories in the space. Each "part" sits serenely on another simple part that we call "table." The whole design, a perfect example of the differentiation of parts, is nearly archetypal in its simplicity.   *—Sarah*

inside without interruption, supported by a simple post that also serves as the door jamb on both sides of the door. There's a complete blurring of the boundary that we would normally call the exterior wall.

Several other blurring mechanisms have been used by the architect to bring the outside in, like the water feature that runs through the house. Though each space is completely enclosed on each side by solid walls, there's always light from above, giving another reference to the outside.

In a tiny pocket garden off the master bathroom (left), the deep soaking tub also serves as a pool that is visible from the bed. Natural light from the skylight above cascades down the wall. A reflecting wall surface like this makes an otherwise dark side of the house radiant and inviting.

All of these elements combine to create an environment for living that's so dramatically unlike our normal understanding of house and garden that it may not strike you as a house at all. But it's the essence of the Japanese term *katei*—wonderful architecture, wonderful landscaping, and in combination, a wonderful place to live.   *—Sarah*

A stone wall, softened by a bed of perennials, marks this territory of home. Another line—this time a reverse curve—of stepping stones meanders across the lawn before it breaks through a hedge of blue hydrangeas and signals the entrance to the front door.

The Territory of Home

Vacation homes are often stripped-down versions of our everyday houses, mirroring the simple life we seek when we take time off from the workaday world. This dwelling follows that rule of thumb—straightforward and uncomplicated, yet elegant in all its details. A second home for a retired couple and their family, the project was designed to accommodate their casual summer lifestyle while remaining easy to use and maintain as they grew older. This Sengekontacket Pond residence is also a study in how simple but effective a good landscape journey can be.

The first stage of the journey is simply getting to this home on Martha's Vineyard. Travelers battle the highway traffic to Cape Cod, then take an hour-long ferry ride to the island. Once there, they wend their way down the narrow Vineyard roads until the macadam becomes a sandy track. Another turn brings visitors into the woods,

NOT SO BIG INSIDE OUT

Both Julie and I loved the simplicity of this house and landscape. Though the property is expansive, both architect and landscape architect used restraint in engaging the land. There's an understated and relaxed feeling that emanates from this simple composition of forms. The focus here is on the basic elements of structure—walls on the outside, posts and beams within—and these have been used as the primary aesthetic statement, making the place at once elegant and easy to maintain. —Sarah

and suddenly there's the house. It's a cottage that one can look right through to the pond beyond. Inside, visitors are greeted by views of the meadow and water on the other side. Home again.

This voyage from the outside world to the inner sanctuary, from profane to sacred, is at the heart of every good journey. When leaving behind one world for another, the paths travelers take —highways, roads, lanes, or tracks—help intensify a feeling of anticipation: the longing for home. A good designer can choreograph this experience on your land. In this case, landscape architect Kris Horiuchi cut a new driveway through the old forest, terminating it in a gravel parking court that is defined by a freestanding run of stone wall. This masonry divider signals the ending of the vehicular journey and the beginning of one by foot. Located at the

V **This house is both open and sheltered— the exposed meadow landscape slopes down to the Sengekontacket Pond on one side, and a forest of scrub pines and oaks protects the other.**

V **This simple design vocabulary results in a coherent landscape of home. Banks of bright red windows, weathered wood siding, and stone foundation walls are the building blocks of this home, where the landscape shows equal restraint.**

< By changing the style, dimension, and direction of the paths around your house, you can make distinctions about how they are used. In this case, family members use a path of cut bluestone to enter the mudroom while guests take the more formal stepping-stone path to the front door.

edge of the pitch pine forest, the house defines the transition between woodland and meadow, and marks the beginning of the journey's end.

The Natural and the Sublime

An irregular path of native fieldstone passes through the wall from the gravel parking lot, signaling the entry into the territory of home. The stone wall and the U-shaped house enclose a garden court that is protected from ever-present coastal winds. Inside, a perennial border thrives in the full sun. An arc of flowering shrubs extends around the parking area and leads the eye to the main entrance, reinforcing the feeling of being in a protected place. On the pond side, a large circle of lawn surrounds the house, marking the more cultivated landscape off from that of the wilder meadow.

∧ Shutters that emphasize the vernacular style of the house are a practical solution for a waterfront home. In the off-season, they are pulled closed when the nor'easters batter Martha's Vineyard.

< A circle of lawn is mown out of the wildflower meadow to define the realm of the house and provide a play space around it. The meadow adds color and texture, and it is perfect for chasing fireflies on a summer night.

Pond

Meadow

Grass circle

Screened porch

Deck

Garden court

Circular walk

Garage

Parking

∧ Altering the grading around mature trees is a delicate business. Here, a pine is encircled by a stone retaining wall, its height chosen to maintain the original grade at the base of the tree.

∧ Rafter tails extend about 3 ft. from the façade of the house, breaking up light and casting shadows in the heat of the summer.

Vernacular Inspirations
Both the architecture and the designed landscape recall the site's agricultural past. Instead of imposing a single large mass upon the delicate landscape, architect Mark Hutker conceived of the project as a series of small buildings, using shed forms clad in weathered cedar that reference the simple structures characteristic of New England farm outbuildings. Traditional shutters that actually close to ward off inclement weather combine with wooden trellises, or sun screens, that radiate from the fascia, offering shading from the heat of the sun. A screened porch keeps insects at bay and offers the quiet of an outdoor away room for the family when all members are in residence.

Traditional landscape materials were also used: stone walls, fieldstone pavers, and granite posts, all of which reinforce the connection of the new house to the area's agrarian history.

A former sheep pasture, the 3-acre property is now dominated by drifts of native coastal vegetation, including red cedar, bayberry, viburnum, huckleberry, highbush blueberry, beach plum, and native grasses and wildflowers. Along with the vernacular style of the house, these native plantings echo the homegrown quality of the entire property.

Designing Stepping-Stone Paths

Stepping stones were used in traditional Japanese gardens to keep strollers from sullying their footwear in the mud. In our contemporary landscapes, they make a versatile path that allows you to choreograph where visitors walk, how fast they move, what they look at, and how they feel as they stroll. Stepping stones can be set several inches above the ground, at grade, or even sunken so that a mower can move across them. The stones should be set at least 3 in. apart to accommodate the average gait, and the forms of stones in sequence should usually marry with each other in a yin-yang fashion.

Generally, strollers cast their eyes downward when walking on stepping stones. It helps to break up the left-right, left-right pacing underfoot by occasionally placing one large stone for both feet. Standing on this "pivot point," a person walking on it will be able to look up and view where he or she is going next. This is a good opportunity to place a garden feature nearby, such as a stone lantern or a beautiful plant. You can use two stepping stones together, as Kris Horiuchi did here, to signal that a change is about to take place—here, a step up onto a deck.

—*Julie*

< A deck spans the entire pond side of the house, creating a transitional space between house and landscape. Nearby, an open framework of posts and beams extends the home's structure.

outside
| parallels |

Expressed Structure

HERE YOU CAN see how one building system—the stone wall—expresses its structure as an element of the landscape. Reminiscent of the old stone fences that were built to keep animals within bounds, these walls look more contemporary, built of quarried slag rock rather than the rounded boulders found locally.

The same material and technique, using hidden mortar joints, is at work in a circular wall around a tree and for the facing stones on concrete foundation walls and the chimneys. Expressing the structure of stone brings the sense of unity and clarity to this home's design.   *—Julie*

The Process of Entering

One of the most satisfying aspects of this home is its gracious and welcoming sequence of entry places and events along the way, from the movement through the low courtyard wall to the meandering stepping-stone path across the courtyard to the covered entryway—still outside, but under the protection of the roof—and finally inside the house to what I call the "receiving place." Here you have an immediate sense of what the rest of the house will be like. You experience the solid but warm embrace of the timber-frame structure and wood ceiling, and you are simultaneously beckoned into the main living area by the broad windows on the opposite side of the house.

This entering process plays a number of important roles. First and foremost, it should make you feel happy to be home. Second, it should make guests feel welcome and give them the sense that they are going to be well taken care

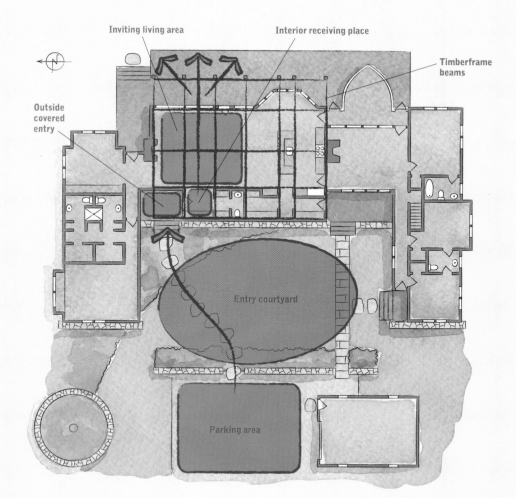

Inviting living area

Interior receiving place

Timberframe beams

Outside covered entry

Entry courtyard

Parking area

of here. And third, it should give everyone who enters a place to transition from the public realm they are leaving to the much more private and intimate realm they are joining. The shape and scale of this receiving place is just right, allowing you to stand for a few seconds and catch your breath, readjust to the new surroundings, and prepare to engage in the experiences offered by the home's interior.

—Sarah

Expressed Structure

COMPOSED OF THREE simple gables reminiscent of the familiar forms of local barns, the house has an informal, cabinlike layout, with most of the living space contained in the primary center building and bedrooms housed in the two flanking wings. Like the older barns of the area, the structure of the center building is a timber frame.

The posts and beams express an aesthetic unto themselves. The exposed wood, while providing structural support, is beautiful in its own right. It's both rustic and interesting to look at. Posts and beams also visually divide the interior into "rooms," lending order to otherwise open space. You can see the locations of the main beams on the floor plan (left). *—Sarah*

Gateways create pausing places in a landscape, where visitors stand between public and private space. An iron archway beckons to a brick path leading to the new front entry.

The World behind the Walls

When they were married some 40 years ago, these homeowners bought a 1920s hunting lodge set on a wooded lot in a Boston suburb. Like so many structures of its day, the house, unfortunately, turned its back on its setting, here one overlooking a lovely pond. In 1995, inspired by the villas of Tuscany, the couple hired architect Abigail Campbell-King to open the house up to its view of the pond, add more space, create a sense of flow, and allow for entertaining with ease. She designed a garage with an office suite above and a new kitchen and dining room oriented to face the pond. As construction began on the addition, I was brought on board to design the landscape. Together, the owners and I worked to anchor the house to its site and knit its parts into a coherent whole.

NOT SO BIG INSIDE OUT

So many homes sit on beautiful pieces of land, but neither the house nor the landscape is designed to take full advantage of the site's potential. That was the case with this home until the homeowners hired an architect and landscape designer—Julie—to help them reveal the beauty that lay hidden by walls and tree limbs. Today, the home is an extraordinary example of what's possible when designers collaborate to make the most of what's already there. —*Sarah*

> The couple added natural light to their new living space with a skylight. Here, the dining room feels brighter than the shady hemlock grove it looks upon.

∧ The focal point from the dining room is a serene pond where autumn colors reflect across its surface. This view is a surprise that can't be seen until one moves through to the back of the house.

Today, the couple's home feels as though it's bursting forth into the landscape through each of its many openings. Reoriented to face the water, windows cover every wall along its L-shaped perimeter on the pond side. The renovated kitchen and dining room nestle in the center of the addition, where a skylight illuminates an oblong banquet table. French doors open onto to a grove of hemlock trees that have been carefully pruned to allow views through to the water below. The many glass doors along the perimeter of the house allow the couple generous access to the outside—to walk along paths, entertain on the overlook, or sit at the breakfast terrace—or to feel connected to the outdoors by borrowing the views from their dining room-window wall.

Overlooking the World
We are drawn to overlooks because they feel both exhilarating and dangerous. Here, I created three important overlooks: the threshold stones that look out on the pond from the kitchen/dining-room addition; the party terrace that looks across a sloping garden of ornamental grasses behind a semi-

V A breakfast terrace of quarried granite stands poised above the pond that is spied through carefully pruned hemlock trees. Stone in many forms was used as the unifying material around this European-style home.

circular sitting wall of stone; and the breakfast nook that sits just above the pond, large enough for a teak table and two chairs. In order to lend a feeling of safety to a high overlook, it helps to create a parapet, or turned-up edge, like the sitting wall of stone we built at the terrace. The couple enjoys looking down from their high prospect, an important part of creating their particular landscape of home.

ALL AROUND THE HOUSE

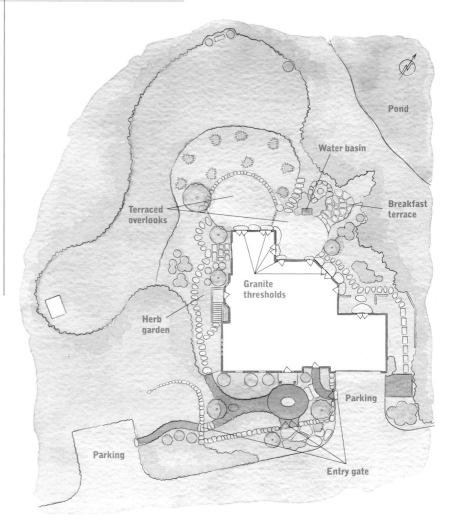

Pond

Water basin

Breakfast terrace

Terraced overlooks

Granite thresholds

Herb garden

Parking

Parking

Entry gate

> Granite thresholds take the place
of foundation plantings around the
base of this home, acting as a step
between building and landscape.
Beyond, a terrace of bluestone set
diagonally to the house unites the
different outdoor spaces.

∧ Two water features are in view at the
same time: the neighboring pond and a
carved granite basin. The latter provides
an architectural counterpoint to the
rounded boulder that flanks it.

On the Threshold

Large granite chunks act like mini
overlooks at each entry. These thresholds sit a half foot above the
garden level, rooting the house to the ground. Looking out from
the den, your eye tumbles from the threshold of granite to the
bluestone overlook, to the granite breakfast terrace, and to the softer
pine needles, the shoreline, and finally the dark liquid expanse of
pond. This waterfall effect is just one of the ways that the house and
additions welcome the lush gardens and views.

< Large granite stepping stones lead through a garden of
sensory pleasures: the owner's herb and cutting garden. Here,
the south-facing slope offers a place for roses, Russian sage,
oregano, rosemary, and even tomatoes to flourish.

Using one material in a variety of different shapes and forms brings coherence to a design, both inside and out. I used the granite thresholds to link indoor and outdoor spaces. The same threshold stone is also used as the paving stone for the breakfast nook, for all the landscape steps down the slope, and for stepping stones through the herb garden. A further variation combines granite with brick pavers in the front courtyard and granite with bluestone pavers on the party terrace.

Embracing the Realm

The land is surrounded by masses of mature rhododendron bushes and giant hemlock trees, giving it privacy from the adjacent roads that border two sides of the site. To give them even more privacy, I decided to build walls around the front entrance to the house, hiding the beauty within. Walls cascade in curving steps along the roadway and around the corner of the driveway, bestowing a lyrical quality to the solid structure. Inside, I created an oval-shaped courtyard of brick and granite. An American dogwood tree graces the corner; its blossoms are replicated in the wrought-iron window carved into the high wooden entry gates. When you embrace your land, or realm, by enclosing it with a wall, fence, hedge, or plantings, it effectively makes a home feel private, secure, yours.

THE LANDSCAPE OF HOME

A Continuously Changing Path

Every successful garden journey links different events along a continuously changing path. Here, the spatial journey allows the house and garden to be revealed in sequence. Underfoot, brick becomes granite, granite becomes bluestone, and bluestone changes from a random rectangular pattern to a diagonal pattern as it modulates out from inside the house.

A granite "welcome mat" facing the entry vestibule forms the center of a series of concentric bands of brick radiating outward (see p. 111). At the end of the same courtyard, a circular pattern in brick marks the spot where three paths come together. One links this brick circle to the oval granite welcome mat. Another path leads off to an herb garden around the south side of the house, where the large granite chunks reappear, this time as stepping stones. The last guides you up some steps and through an arch of wrought iron that directs

you to the street. Paths, like gateways, can help guide us on our garden journeys, making sense of the landscape of home.   —Julie

outside

parallels

Gateways

Psychological Breathing Space

Have you ever noticed how awkward the transitions between inside and outside are in most houses? There's typically a poorly designed step, ranging from 3 in. to 8 in. in height, and there's no thought given to the experience of moving from inside to out. Just as with the process of entering, where a "receiving place" is desirable to allow a shift of personality from public to private self, the same is true as we move out into the landscape. We need a place to stand for a moment and appreciate the qualities of this new realm we're moving into. Such a place provides us a "psychological breathing space."

The large slabs of granite at each doorway provide delightful breathing spaces, almost like miniature balconies, from which to survey the garden before committing to exploring it further. Their uneven shape associates them strongly with the natural world beyond the walls of the house, but their broad, flat surfaces invite people to move easily from inside to outside realms and back again. Collectively, they also provide a base for the entire addition, grounding it and giving it an organic, natural feel, as though the house were built on bedrock.

In a similar way, at the front entry, there's a palpable sense that you are entering a special place as you step through the gate connecting inner and outer worlds—street on one side, inner courtyard on the other. Directly aligned with

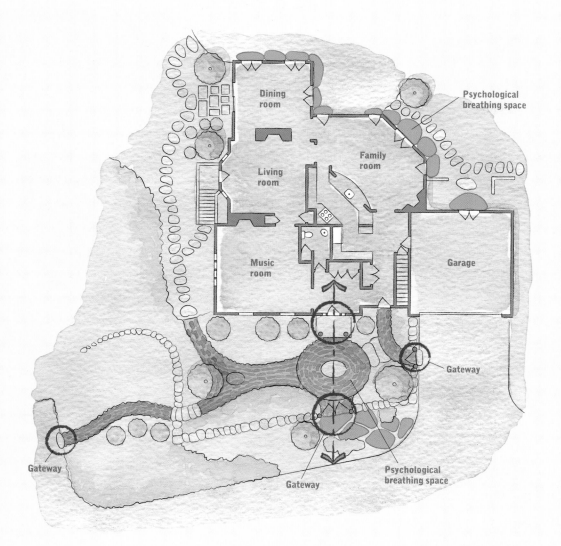

Dining room

Living room

Family room

Psychological breathing space

Music room

Garage

Gateway

Gateway

Gateway

Gateway

Psychological breathing space

the front door, one's gaze is drawn inevitably to the granite circle ahead, surrounded by its radiating crown of brick. The entire composition centers and grounds you, and, as a visitor, you can't help but stop here and take note of the house and its lovely surroundings. Though there are no walls to define the place, the power of the pattern itself is enough to root you to it for a moment, inviting you to stand right here, and look around. —*Sarah*

Gateways

A DOORWAY or framed opening is the interior equivalent of a gateway, and just like its exterior counterpart, it designates and celebrates the transition between one place and the next. The front doorway is the most important gateway of all because it provides the primary point of access between inside and outside realms.

In this home, the front door, with its flanking sidelights and covered stoop, is aligned with the front gateway at the entrance to the property,

so the sense of entering is accentuated and made a little more formal. On departure, the alignment draws attention to the entry to the outer world. In conjunction, the two gateways heighten the powerful experiences of coming and going. —*Sarah*

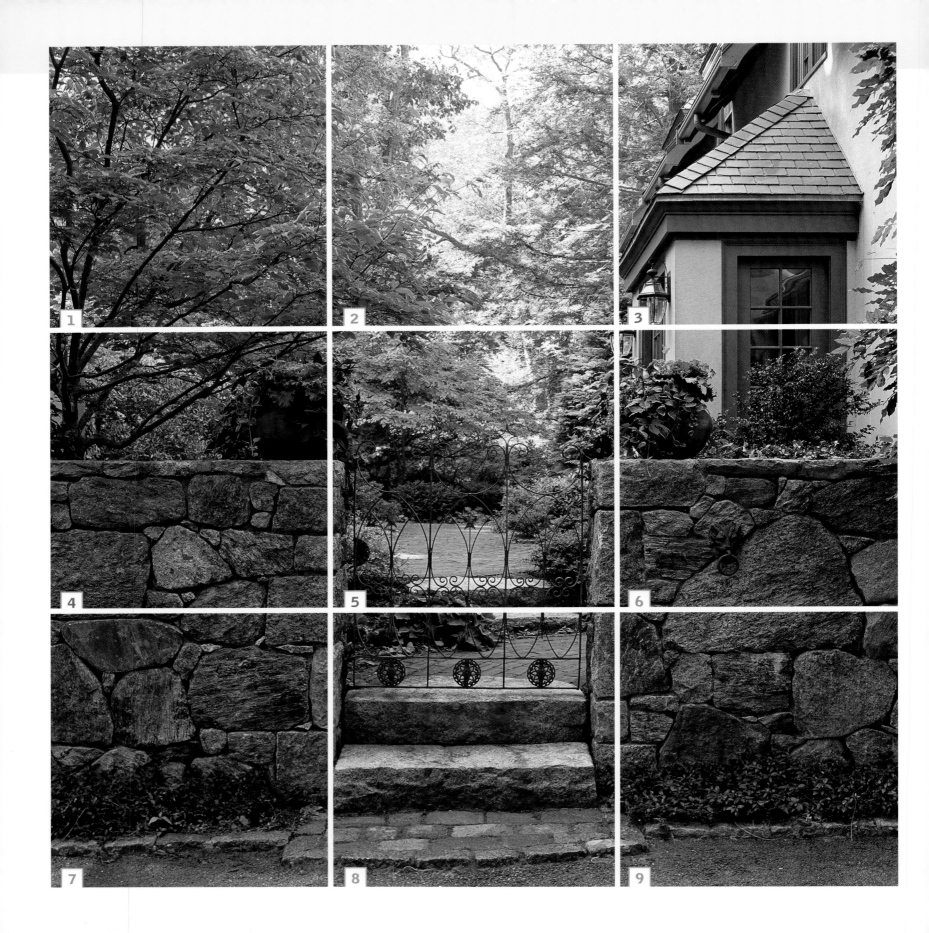

An openwork wrought-iron gateway breaks the solidity of the handsome granite walls around the house. Beyond, the path is windy, narrow, and more informally planted than the entry that sits a few steps above it. These clues all indicate which door to go to: friends and family to this casual "back door," and newcomers to the front gate.

1	2	3
4	5	6
7	8	9

5 **By creating a pivot point** at their center, these three paths were brought together in a subtle but recognizable way. This circle of bricks acts as a point of decision, no matter from which way you come.

4 **These superbly crafted** granite walls were built by an Italian stonemason to match an older existing wall nearby. An orange-berried scarlet fire thorn (*Pyracantha coccinea*) has been espaliered, or trained, to grow flat against this upright wall, enlivening it and giving the entry court a European feel.

3 **Here, a father** and son stonemason team confirms that building walls is an art form. Each stone is interlocked for resilience and strength, as well as aesthetic value.

113

Connecting indoors and outdoors allows the sense of home

to extend beyond the walls.

Frames

Linking the Inside with the Out

Frames

Designed to extend the presence of the house into the landscape, this deck seems to float above the lawn. Even the vines look like they're barely touching the nearly invisible wire fence that supports them.

Living Lightly on the Land

If there were a corollary to "Not So Big" in landscape design, it would be what I call "living lightly on the land." This principle can be translated as design in several ways: You can downsize the amount of space you use for living and gardening, use sustainable materials and techniques, or design with an eye for economy and simplicity. Architects John Maier and Ulrike Zelter chose to live lightly in their 1,300-sq.-ft. duplex in Austin, Texas, taking a 1950s house with a big yard and creating a home that is small, simple, and sustainable.

Built in an area of cottages and bungalows, this modest home contains two living units. Originally, a path led to a centered, gabled stoop that provided shared entry. This bisected lawn seemed meager to the new owners, who decided their tenants should have the front yard for their use. The couple then built a generous porch along the

NOT SO BIG INSIDE OUT

This house is a great example of using a simple, limited, and inexpensive palette of materials to accomplish a sense of serenity and delight without having a lot of space inside or out. Like several of the houses in this book, it's no accident that this is an architect couple's own home. They know the value of good design and understand how to implement it to maximum effect.
    —*Sarah*

front of the house that was shifted toward the tenants' unit. The front walk remained aligned in the center. This overcame the "duplex symmetry" of the house, giving it a more homelike appearance. It also gave the rental unit another 200 sq. ft. of living space. Large concrete slabs, lined up with the side-by-side front doors, provide a playful front walk for both units. The whole is as carefully composed as a Japanese garden, but created out of modern materials.

Back to the Front   Choosing to locate their entry at the rear of the site gave the architects privacy from their tenants and neighbors, an expanded backyard, and immediate access to their carport. Desiring more connection between inside and outside, they located two pairs of glass sliding doors that open out onto an ipé deck. Echoing the planter box detail that they used in the front, the couple built two steel boxes that terrace down from the deck onto a lawn bounded by a wide strip of knippa stone—a local gravel. The simplicity of these materials brings presence and design clarity to the form of the house.

∧ Two doors greet visitors as they pick their way up the front walk of concrete slabs. The very first pavers indicate by their placement that two families live there.

< At first glance (far left), the front yard looks like others nearby, but closer inspection reveals a thoughtfully designed juxtaposition of materials. This couple peeled back the lawn to expose a sidewalk of gravel and composed their welcome path of sidewalk-size slabs of concrete. A closer look reveals a sheltered retreat: Red canvas butterfly chairs sit on the front deck (left), which is covered by a corrugated roof and supported by the slimmest of columns bringing a tropical flavor to this comfy hangout.

> This architect couple designed their home to reflect their desire for economy and sustainability. The carport/workshop roof floats with only the barest of supports, and a wide wooden wall moves on rollers across a track.

ALL AROUND THE HOUSE

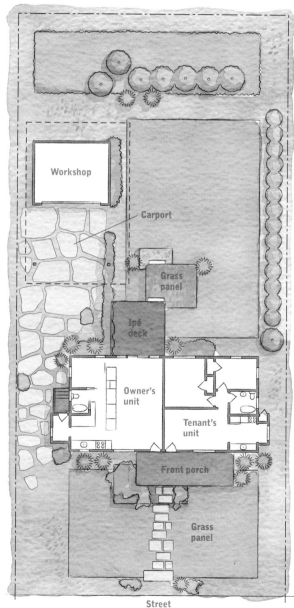

Workshop

Carport

Grass panel

Ipé deck

Owner's unit

Tenant's unit

Front porch

Grass panel

Street

Privacy Without Walls

While constructing masonry walls or high fences at the property line gives a feeling of seclusion and privacy from nearby neighbors, you can create a similar feeling of sanctuary by the use of screens, borders, and buildings. At the edges of their gravel border, John and Ulrike planted tall evergreens to give privacy to the yard without having to build a fence. Enclosed by steel mesh panels, the workshop is further integrated into the garden by allowing the panels to rust and covering them with passionflower vine. A similar screen is used to give privacy at the back deck, where evergreen clematis grows on horizontal wires that allow air and light through.

Inside Out

The owners designed their unit from the inside out. They wanted a more spacious living area with better light and a stronger connection to their backyard landscape. So they removed all the walls except those surrounding the bathroom and divided the living areas with large, multifunctional cabinets. They also chose to repeat certain colors throughout: spring green walls that echo the grass and plantings outside, complemented by a rich red that washes walls and door frames and is found outside on the canvas seats of the butterfly chairs.

< The design vocabulary inside is consistent with the outside. An interior door, painted red, seems to float in space with no obvious hinges attaching it to a frame.

The couple's choice to live lightly on the land is supported by design details that create the sensation of levity. Each different material or element seems to float separately in space. As seen from the back corner of the property, the lawn floats next to a plane of gravel bounded by steel edging. The carport roof floats out over the lawn, seemingly supported by only the slimmest of steel columns. A grass panel floats above the lawn, edged by a band of black wood to form a turf step down into the landscape. A single rectangle of concrete—the first step off the cantilevered deck—seems to float upon the grass panel. This home shows just how one might execute a sustainable, economical design that's also a thing of beauty.

< Everything in its place: A picnic area at the rear of the property offers a long view across the lawn to the house.

∧ The raised panel of grass projects above the lawn and connects the deck to the backyard. A third raised rectangle is seen in the roof of the carport/workshop, completing the composition.

Recycling Materials

The Maier-Zelter home demonstrates ways that house and landscape design can be elegant and sustainable. The couple sought to reuse existing materials wherever possible. They built with refurbished steel casement windows and cedar sidewall shakes, and they constructed a new table and benches from Douglas fir framing material. Outside, they cut concrete walkways that surrounded the house into tile-size chunks for stepping-stones. From the badly fissured concrete driveway, they created a new oversize "cracked ice" patterned driveway that lies in a bed of knippa stone and plants.

Landscape designer Jon Ahrens and the owners also chose to create a low-maintenance garden using xeriscaping principles, which involve creating sustainable landscapes that conserve water and protect the environment. In urban areas of Texas, about a quarter of the water supply is used for landscape and garden watering. Good planning and design, careful soil analysis, limiting turf areas or using drought-tolerant grasses that don't need irrigation, along with appropriate plant selection, efficient irrigation, use of mulches to hold in moisture, and appropriate maintenance, all help preserve water in arid states.

—*Julie*

outside
parallels

Floating Objects

IN THIS HOME, each material—metal, wood, concrete, plant, or grass—looks as though it is floating or weightless, hovering above the surfaces around it. At the owner's entrance, a metal roof floats above the walls, its structure invisible from the garden. Below, the ipé deck drifts above the ground plane, seemingly attached only at the house and cantilevered far into the garden

space. Two poured concrete slabs, their white color standing in stark contrast to the dark stain of the deck and steel planter adjacent to them, seem to hang above the grass and gravel plinths on which they sit. Even the planters, separated from other materials by color, texture, and edging of steel, seem to float above the lawn panel. —*Julie*

Doing Double Duty

Double-duty function is at the core of what makes this home work so well with such limited spatial resources. Julie has described how the carport not only provides a place to shelter the cars from the elements, but also helps enclose the garden, protecting it from neighboring properties and even from a view to the cars themselves. This is a perfect example of one element doing double duty.

So, too, is the front porch design. It does double duty by creating a sense of entry for the house as a whole while quietly offering the tenants of the second unit a bit more space to call their own. Had the design of this porch been considered only as a shelter for the entry doors themselves, there'd be no double duty. It's the extension of the porch in front of the tenants' living-room picture window that makes it work. This is clearly their territory, and not that of the primary unit.

On the interior of the house, you see the same attitude brought to bear in the design of the pod of space described at right. When the doors are closed, it looks like a piece of boldly colored furniture. But when it's open, it adds alcoves of activity space that you don't always want to have visible, but which are very

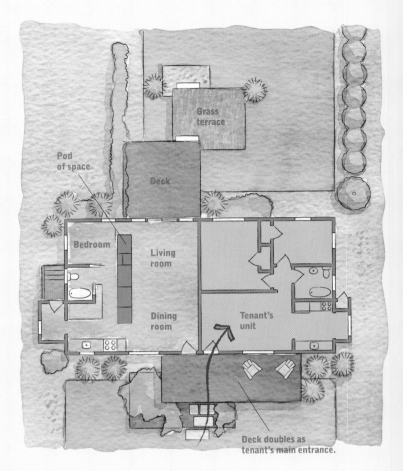

Deck doubles as tenant's main entrance.

Floating Objects

INSIDE A HOME, you can use "floating objects" to make a space look significantly bigger than it is. Instead of separating rooms with walls that extend to the ceiling, you can create what I call a "pod of space"—an object that contains storage, or a small activity place or utility area. If you look at the floor plan on the facing page, you'll see that instead of a dividing wall between the bathroom and the living area, the couple has employed a pod of space for storage. The ceiling plane extends over top of the pod and beyond the edge of the "room." Your senses perceive that the room you're in is larger than it actually is. The same effect is accentuated by the sides of the pod, which is finished to resemble furniture, rather than a wall.

—Sarah

much needed in a house of this size. In addition to its room-dividing functions, it is also chock full of creative storage. With the sliding panels open, the living area now includes a desk space, the dining table serving as extra layout area. Also hidden behind the sliding doors is storage for stereo equipment and CDs, as well as bedroom closet space, which is accessed from the other side of the pod.

—Sarah

Extending the presence of home into the out-of-doors allows us to witness the elements without actual contact. On still summer evenings, any movement of the air, enjoyed from the back-and-forth rhythm of a rocking chair or porch swing, is refreshing.

Easy Living

Down South, people just know how to live out-of-doors. To take advantage of a warm and humid climate, they have created a network of indoor-outdoor places for enjoying their family, their neighbors, and their environment. Porches, screened rooms, arbors, and formal gardens are among these spaces—attached to the house yet part of the landscape. They are transitional places that combine home with garden and encourage privacy or sociability, depending upon one's mood.

Husband-and-wife designers Ken Troupe and Cally Heppner got the mood just right on their property in Beaufort, South Carolina. Sitting out on their covered front porch on a sultry summer evening, the couple can stir up a breeze in their side-by-side rockers or on their hanging porch swing. From their perch 4 ft. above the street, they can nestle back against the house or call out

NOT SO BIG INSIDE OUT

This house exhibits such a beautiful integration of landscape and building, with the two aspects interconnecting throughout the property, that Julie and I instantly knew it belonged in this book. Its parts extend out into the site, where plantings grow abundantly over and through them to create a sense of cloistered sanctuary—proof that you don't need acres to attain a sense of seclusion.   —*Sarah*

< When the source for this charming bronze statue is turned off, the central water feature becomes a reflecting pool, complete with water lilies floating on the surface.

to a neighbor passing by—it's a perfect vantage point that offers both prospect and refuge at the same time. The porch also acts as an outdoor entry vestibule. It's the place where a visitor might dust him- or herself off before knocking. Secluded and secure, it is a special transitional space that makes occupants—whether inhabitants or visitors—feel completely comfortable.

Serene on the Side

Another porch, this one screened, wraps the side and back of the house and fronts on the formal side garden. Designed to extend an insect-free indoor-outdoor living space into the landscape, this screened room adds a special dimension to everyday life. The high-gabled roof and ganged window screens veil and soften the eastern morning light. Jutting out into the landscape like a dock over water, the screened porch, along with a pair of towering live oaks, serves to break down the side garden into two parts.

A formal garden, complete with circular brick fountain and semicircular matching path, occupies the side yard. Its strong geometries focus the eye, creating a literal center with a dynamic focal point—a fountain of water that occupies the center of the brick pool. Traditional southern plantings like boxwood trees, azaleas, and dogwood trees soften the edges of this landscaped outdoor room.

ALL AROUND THE HOUSE

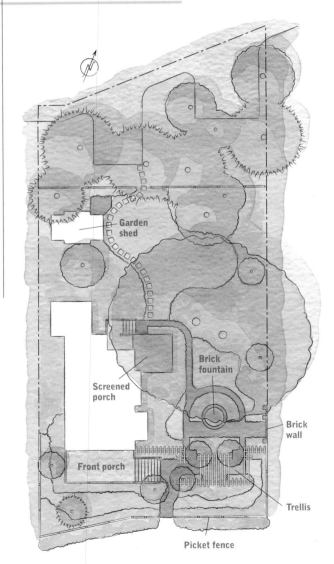

Garden shed

Brick fountain

Screened porch

Brick wall

Front porch

Trellis

Picket fence

< The couple chose their lot for the two majestic live oak trees that shade the whole backyard.

< Here you can see how to literally extend the presence of home by building a framework of trellising and screens as part of your landscape.

< *Verbena canadensis* "Homestead Purple" sews itself freely in front of the picket fence along the lane. Behind the fence, confederate jasmine vine blooms white to form a dense hedge.

Screening Out the Public

Since the house is located within yards of two public streets, privacy is a major concern. A sense of separation between the public space of the sidewalk and the private yard has been created with a 4-ft.-high picket fence. Dense plantings on each side of it add another layer of screening at the base of the house.

To wonderful effect, the owners carefully echoed details, colors, and forms throughout their property. For instance, the pickets in the fence are repeated in the railings that encircle both porches. A tall, carefully pruned pine tree creates privacy on the second-floor porch, playing up the contrast between the stark white building and the soft green plantings that surround it. A decorative trellised gateway and picket fence provide privacy for the back yard, and a brick wall and another fence along the side property line define and enclose the low-maintenance courtyard. With so many delightful sitting places to choose from, this study in gracious Southern living is a place for all to emulate.

< In this neotraditional community, architectural and planning review boards determined that the lots should be small and the façades close to the street to create a close-knit community.

Open Enclosures

When you reside in a neighborhood setting, it's hard to feel good about walling yourself off from others. Callie Heppner and Ken Troupe used what I call "open enclosures" as a means of screening but not separating themselves from view.

Along the street edge, they erected a hall-like wooden post-and-beam structure on which vines grow, and they fastened openwork trellis panels between columns to screen out the street. The couple left out panels to

either side of the central trellis, creating windows into the garden. This composition keeps the sense of neighborliness while firmly defining private from public space.

Callie and Ken also erected handsome piers and in-filled them with a high solid wall flanked by lower openwork screens, all made of the same brick used for the fountain. This solid-open-solid pattern echoes the wooden trellis structures along the street edge, offering privacy yet allowing controlled views in.

—Julie

< Furthering the traditional feeling of this neighborhood is the rear laneway, which means that cars are kept in back. Here, the couple screens the driveway area with a charming trellised gateway and picket fencing.

Moving Toward the Light

OUTSIDE YOUR HOUSE, you can use plantings and built form to lead eye and foot along a path from darkness toward light—a wonderful way of drawing people through a space. Here, Callie and Ken built a pergola that feels private despite its location next to the street and sidewalk.

The long, linear trellis creates a hall-like enclosure to bring privacy to the

side-yard garden. The structure's roof makes a crosshatched shadow on the brick floor. A panel of wooden trellising also creates dappled light and air circulation in this "hallway." At its terminus, the structure is open to the sky and to the street, allowing shafts of light to lead you forward to enjoy the plantings that mark the destination.   —*Julie*

Sequence of Places

Whenever I'm designing a house, I like to think of it not as a set of rooms, but as a sequence of places for the activities of daily life. When I first sit down with clients, I'll ask them to describe for me their mornings, daylight hours, and evenings. This helps to liberate us from the limitations that come with individual room names. A dining room doesn't always have to be for dining, for example. The same thing holds true when designing the garden areas. It's better to use activity descriptions to start with, and label each place as a "porch" or "deck" after that. I can imagine, in planning this home, that the designer couple made something akin to the following list:

Place to sit outside in the evenings and look out over the street—possibly with the ability to talk with passersby. (This function served by the front porch; A.)

Place that's private, shaded, and free of bugs, where we can go to eat or have a drink—needs to be close to kitchen, and should have a secluded view to the garden. (This function served by the screened porch; B.)

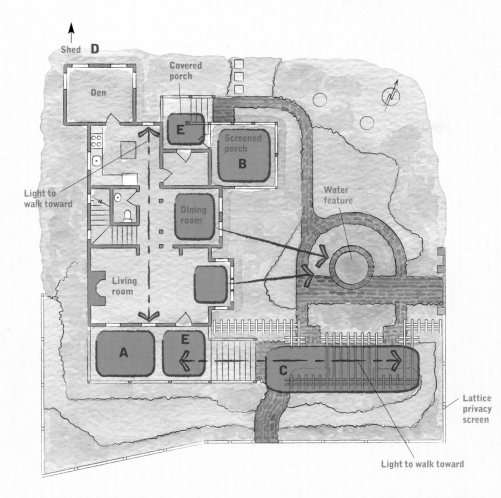

Shed **D**

Covered porch

Den

E

Screened porch **B**

Light to walk toward

Dining room

Water feature

Living room

A   **E**

C

Lattice privacy screen

Light to walk toward

Shaded pathway for strolling in the garden. (This function served by the entry arbor and brick walkways; C.)

Place for storing garden equipment and tools that doesn't shriek "garden shed" when you look at it. (This function served by the shed; D.)

Welcoming entries that are covered from above so those entering have protection from rain. (This function served by the front and rear entry porches; E.)

This list can then be turned into a sequence of outdoor places that are natural extensions of their indoor counterparts.   —*Sarah*

Light to Walk Toward

IT'S IMPORTANT to compose the views connecting activity places so that they will draw you through from one room to the next, engage you. It's clear that at either end of this hallway is a window. Notice how the brightness of the glass area beckons you into the living room, its light reflecting off the hardwood floor, providing a cheerful glow to the room. Remove the window, however, and you have nothing to draw you toward the room.   —*Sarah*

This homeowner's property enjoys only a distant view of the ocean. To provide closer access to water, the architects cantilevered a viewing deck over a small pond, which is built into the ledge that occupies much of this property.

A Landscape of Stone

Manchester-by-the-Sea is a beautiful community on the north shore of Boston that sits right on the Atlantic Ocean. The presence of water is palpable in the atmosphere, in the views, and in the psyche of its residents. Olga and Ken have lived in different houses here over the years, finally settling in this contemporary stucco home perched high on a hillside of ledge, with just one view to the water—from the breakfast nook in the kitchen. The architects, Gitta Robinson and Richard Grisaru, oriented the whole house around this one small view and further satisfied Olga's love of water by incorporating a small pond into the house design.

The pond stands as a wonderful integration of landscape and architecture: It is the link between the two and the focal point of each. Perched atop a massive rock formation, the living-room wing

NOT SO BIG INSIDE OUT

Here's a house that uses exterior elements to root the house firmly to its hilly site and to set the stage for the experiences of the interior. Both of us loved the interplay of water and stone, as well as the contrast between the organic feel of the outside and the clean crispness and simple elegance of the interior. Through these contrasts, outside and inside environments support and enhance each other. —*Sarah*

merges with the landscape through a series of layers from inside to out. At the center stands the hearth, used as a room divider between living and music rooms. Moving outward, an open hallway brings circulation to the perimeter of the space, opening onto a narrow deck under the eaves that sits about a foot above a rocky ledge. Inscribed into that ledge is the pond, with recirculating water, carp, and water plants that grow in the crevices.

What truly brings the site and its building into harmony is the 20-ft. concrete wall that emerges from within the building. It acts as a fulcrum against which the house "cranks," or shifts direction, in order to sit more evenly on the ledge. It brings the interior of the house out into the landscape, firmly establishing the presence of home. And most important, the wall acts as a point of focus for a waterfall that splashes onto a large, flat stone in the pond.

∧ The stone terrace fits right into the space between house and ledge. In the foreground, another concrete aggregate wall emerges from within the house to provide a privacy screen for the hot tub.

ALL AROUND THE HOUSE

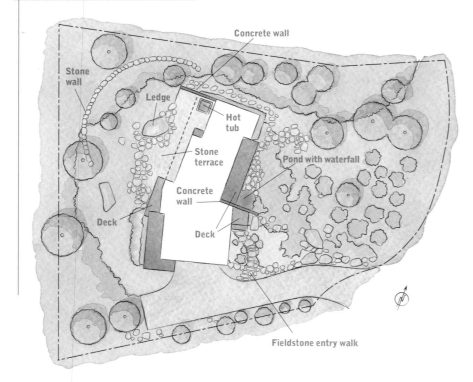

Concrete wall

Stone wall

Ledge

Hot tub

Stone terrace

Pond with waterfall

Concrete wall

Deck

Deck

Fieldstone entry walk

Wall by Design The concrete wall that penetrates house and landscape serves one other important purpose: It provides a strong visual separation between what feels like the private backyard and the public front yard, where the front door is, just behind the other side of the wall. Visitors arrive at the two-story house and proceed up a slope of fieldstone to reach the front door. Stones confront you every step of the way, a foreshadowing of the reeflike sheets of ledge on the other side of the wall. The rocky entry steps are softened by creeping juniper and thyme, which cascade from the cracks.

Around the property, Olga used rocks as a retaining element in order to create level ground on her otherwise uneven site. Setting them against an upward-facing slope, she created planting pockets for a rock garden that she enjoys from her deck. Granite stepping-stones lead back to a low sitting wall of cut stone taken from a nearby quarry. The wall forms an arc that appears to hold back the forest so that light and air may fill the site.

Where the stone emerges as ledge, the landscape is interrupted by smooth drumlins of granite. Nestled next to the ledge, a stone terrace mediates between house and garden. Not far away sits a hot tub, protected from northerly winds by a second freestanding concrete wall. The masterly use of walls, stone, wood, and water each serve to extend the presence of this home.

< Floor-to-ceiling sliding doors dissolve the walls between inside and outside. The clean lines of the architecture stand in stark contrast to the water garden.

Building Ponds

A small water feature like a pond or reflecting pool is a focal point that offers a surface of ever-changing patterns, reflections, and movement. Ponds require certain conditions in order to function and work aesthetically in a landscape. First, you need to locate a pond in a spot that enjoys full sun and occupies level land. When constructing the pond, make sure that you compact the soil beneath the pond bed, use a liner that holds water effectively—either butyl rubber, concrete, or tamped clay—and design the edge around the pond so that it has a natural effect, rather than as a string of lined-up stones. When you incorporate a ledge, as was done here, make sure to plug holes so that the water doesn't leak out into the crevices over time.

—Julie

outside
| p a r a l l e l s |

Overlook From Above

HIGH VANTAGES in a landscape affect us in contradictory ways. We are drawn to the edge of an overlook, excited to see the view, yet we are fearful of falling. One way of counterbalancing our trepidation is to turn up the edge itself by creating a parapet, a railing, or a balustrade. Here, the

wooden deck is protected by a wood-and-steel railing, set at the 36-in. height required by the building code. The freestanding stone wall, while not actually set at the edge of a high vantage, acts like a parapet, separating the natural forest from the more domesticated lawn and garden. —Julie

Window Positioning

When a site has a unique view from one location, as this one does, it is well worth designing a spot just for its appreciation. The more frequently used the spot is, the more the view will become a focus of the experience of the home. The architects for this home, Gitta Robinson and Richard Grisaru, made the kitchen into even more of a focal gathering place than usual by placing the informal eating area in the best location to glimpse the ocean. Both the place and the view from it become a destination that you look forward to, and by wrapping the corner with windows, it's as though you are projected out into the view or on the deck of a ship.

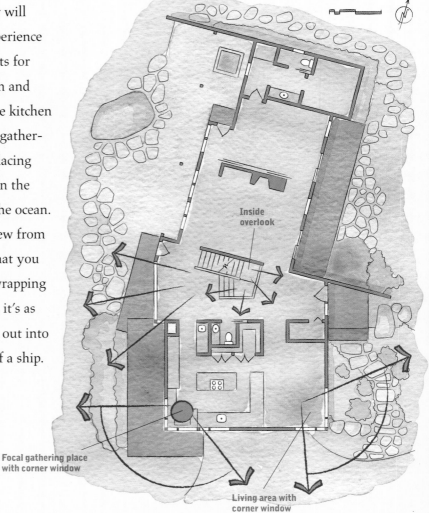

Inside overlook

Focal gathering place with corner window

Living area with corner window

Overlook From Above

IN THE INTERIOR of the house, an overlook, such as the stair landing shown here, offers a different perspective from which to appreciate the home. This overlook allows you to experience front and back entries from a single spot. Standing here, you feel as if you are on a stage. In the same way that standing on a hilltop allows you to survey the territory beneath you, a raised platform like this one gives you a place to linger for a moment as you descend the stair and allows a sense of anticipation to take hold within. Although you may not literally think, "I'm excited to go and explore this sequence of places," at a subliminal level, this is the experience. *—Sarah*

In fact, window positioning was an important consideration throughout this house. The owner, an avid gardener, wanted the house to give her visual connection to the surrounding garden, as well as allow her to keep houseplants. Windows in many areas of the house descend all the way to the floor, blurring the distinction between inside and outside, giving an unobstructed view to the deck and woods beyond, and providing lots of light for the plants.

—Sarah

The contrast between inside and outside, hard surfaces and soft, lines and curves, and front and back all come together around the concrete wall that emerges from the house to become part of the landscape. Here, two planes intersect around water: the vertical wall that spills water and the horizontal wooden deck over the pond.

1	2	3
4	5	6
7	8	9

5 **A slit in the metal trough** that sits on top of the concrete wall allows water to splash on a well-placed stone in the pond. The wall was formed with an aggregate—a mixture of pebbles and small pieces of rock that were ground down to reveal their texture and color and to better blend with the natural landscape.

9 **The owner knew** that in order to assemble so many different plants together in one space without creating a jumble, she needed to establish clear edges between planting beds. Here, a tiny triangle of grass acts as terminus for a path while giving distinct boundaries to beds of yellow daylilies, pink roses, and magenta asters.

4 **7** **Stones look best** when they are set deep into the ground so that their undersides are hidden. These granite fieldstone steps fall down the slope like a waterfall; where juniper and thyme creeps over them, they feel well set.

This spacious terrace is the perfect extension of the home. With ample places to relax, vivid plantings that add beauty and privacy, and the gentle bubbling of the garden pool, this area is transformed into a small paradise.

Good Fences

"Good fences make good neighbors"—at this home near Washington, D.C., the old adage certainly holds true. Every inch of the back and side yards has been thoughtfully enclosed, either with walls, fencing, or hedging, to create a series of private outdoor rooms for the family who lives there. These rooms literally bring the inside out into the fresh air and under the stars, offering the family a completely different living experience. Outside, they can grill, dine, entertain, read the paper, and even sunbathe with abandon, since they are secluded by perimeter hedges and fences. In fact, it's a little like a having a summer home attached to your primary residence.

Located on the corner of a busy pedestrian route to the nearby subway station, the house at first glance looks much like other homes built on quarter-acre lots in this leafy Maryland suburb.

NOT SO BIG INSIDE OUT

The home you see here presents the same kinds of challenges that face most homeowners in the inner-ring suburbs: A site that isn't very big, neighbors close at hand, and streets flanking two sides, making privacy both important and difficult to attain. What struck both of us about this property is its simple and effective approach to "room making" beyond the boundaries of the house to create places for everyday living.   —Sarah

∧ Adding a touch of whimsy in a planter by the front door can soften the hardness of the handsome stone wall and steps.

∧ A massive shade tree stands tall over a row of evergreens adding a high privacy screen above the board fence and shielding the entertainment terrace from the street. For people who live on corner lots or busy streets, this level of privacy is essential.

∨ A narrow stepping-stone path suggests an alternative route from the front door to the entertainment terrace, one that winds between trees and through shade-loving ground covers to open, sunny lawn.

Trees shade the street, a handsome magnolia protects the front door, and lawn sweeps up to plantings of shrubs and evergreen ground covers that hide the foundation of the house. But the difference is in the details. Just off the front walk, a stepping-stone path meanders through carefully edged beds of Lenten rose, foamflower, and pachysandra, weaving past stands of birches like a stream that winds through natural woodland, luring visitors in.

Along the way, the path changes from natural fieldstone to square-cut bluestone, heralding the paving material of the terrace that forms the first of a series of outdoor rooms encircling the sides and back of the house. The path continues through an open gateway at the center of a 4-ft.-high wooden fence, offering passersby a glimpse of the realm within. Terminating three steps up, it widens into a large outdoor space for family entertainment.

The World Behind the Wall   When seen from the street, the entertainment terrace is almost completely hidden from view. The fanlike form of a mature tree casts high and wide to bring upper-story privacy. Below it, a tall hedge of evergreens adds

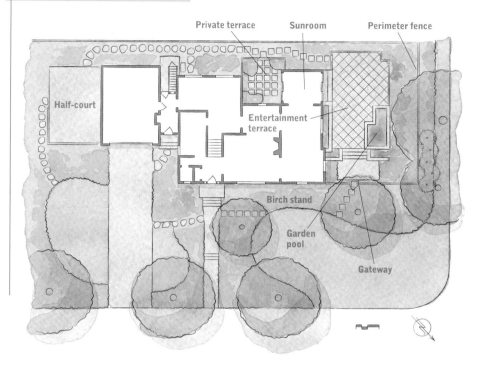

∧ The path crosses through a sea of perennial foamflower in bloom, moves through a wooden gateway, and ascends to the terrace. Here, shade gives way to sun; low becomes high; narrow becomes broad.

another level of screening between the tree's branching structure and a 6-ft. board fence that encloses the back and side yards of the property. Inside is a space large enough to hold a small party tent. Set apart physically and psychically, this world behind the wall becomes a kind of safe zone for the family. The sense of seclusion is further bolstered by a lovely garden pool, built at the corner of the terrace that houses a bubbler, fish, and water lilies.

Designed by landscape architect Sandra Clinton, the terrace is a study in the elegant details that make an enclosed space feel larger than it really is. Every square inch holds value; every corner is revealed. The middle becomes a place for dining and socializing, and the background stays respectfully behind the fence.

Rooms Inside and Out
The rooms inside the McCulloch house are just as carefully designed to relate to the living spaces outside as the outside rooms relate to the interior. Architect Winn Faulkner worked with the family to create an

< A triangular clerestory window above the doors brings the outside into this congenial sunroom. If it were closed in as a wall, the room would feel far smaller, darker, and less open to its environs.

∨ This picture window becomes a central focal point of the living room with its divided panes of glass breaking up the attractive view beyond into smaller fragments, each more interesting than the next.

∧ The narrow passageway between house and lot line beckons visitors to follow, thanks to a slight bend along the way. A deviation like this curve can make all the difference between the unexpected and the predictable.

addition on the side of the house that fronts onto the entertainment terrace. Two small *tempietti*—little templelike rooms with high gabled windows—form matching bookends to a living-room addition in the middle. Each façade offers views onto the terrace. On one end of the quarry-tiled garden room are French doors that open onto the entertainment terrace; the other end steps out onto a private terrace sized just for one person. This enclosed court is the perfect away room, nestled just outside the dining room, offering a quiet zone for reading or reflection.

In the new living-room addition, a large picture window has been subdivided into 16 panes to frame the view to the garden pool, an echo of the 16 squares that form the floor of the outdoor away room. Such attention to detail, as well as the contemporary artwork, floral displays, and furnishings in rooms that open onto one another, make this house comfortable both inside and out.

Private and Public Realms

The term realm describes the environment over which you have influence: the house and land you call your own. People often present a different public and private face to the world and, unconsciously, do the same with their realms. This home presents a public face that is very different than its private side. The expanse of lawn that extends from house to street acts as a visual buffer zone, further screened by the birch trees and ground-cover beds that surround the front façade. The effect is to preserve a certain anonymity for its owners while presenting an attractive face to the street. You can't tell much about who lives here, beyond the fact that they enjoy their privacy and have a handsome front yard.

In this home, you will find out more about who the owners are when you pass through the gate into the realm behind the fence (see p. 140). The ample terrace with multiple seating areas suggests a vibrant place for entertainment and family dining. Multiple containers of plantings and a reflecting pool with lily pads and water plants indicates a private realm that is well tended, loved, and fully enjoyed and appreciated.

—*Julie*

Diagonals

DIAGONALS ENERGIZE, elongate, and expand an area. Like an arrow pointing back into space, a diagonal points to the broadest expanse, making a garden seem bigger than it is. The designers here used bluestone pavers set on the diagonal to give a sense of greater spaciousness and depth to the entertainment terrace (below).

A diagonal can feel, paradoxically, both dangerous and desirable. Our minds are inexorably drawn to follow something at an angle that focuses and expands our sense of depth. Because it's such a dynamic element, a diagonal needs a resolution point at the end, such as a T-intersection to stop its relentless move forward (see the drawing at right).   *—Julie*

The Weaving of Inside and Out

As you move through this house, there's a gradual progression from public to private spaces, and the outdoor terraces are an important part of this sequence. Although the home is ostensibly a set of defined rooms, because the framed openings between the rooms are wide, the interior becomes a sequence of places along a diagonal view as described in the sidebars.

When interior and exterior spaces are designed in conjunction with one another, the views from place to place are composed in such a way that you are as aware of the outdoor "rooms" as the inside ones. Take, for example, the dining room. Seated here, you can see out to the garden in three directions. The window looking into the outdoor away room is centered on the room, so the view here is to a contained space with an intimate feel. Positioned at 90 degrees to this is a view through the sitting room to the terrace and pond

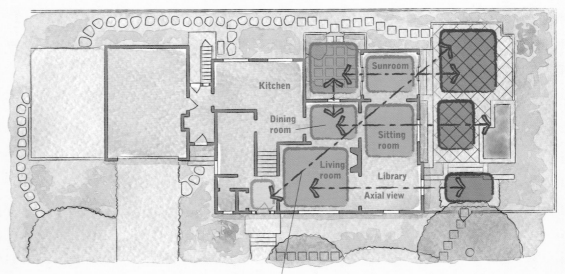

Long diagonal view

Diagonal Views

DIAGONAL VIEWS work the same way in the interior of the house as they do outside. By connecting rooms with wide, framed openings along the diagonal as they are here, the house appears significantly larger than it is. You are able to experience with your eyes the longest enclosed view through the house, in this case from one end of the original living room to the opposite corner of the new sunroom. The view, in this case, is extended further yet—out into the terrace beyond. *—Sarah*

beyond, a more focused view. The third, more oblique view leads the eye along the diagonal through the sunroom windows to the terrace. Each space along the diagonal keeps enticing you toward this outdoor area.

The sunroom itself becomes an interior bridge between two outdoor sitting places—one the most public and expansive, the other much more private and contained. It's a flow-through space with sliding doors that can open wide to the entertainment terrace on one side and the outdoor away room on the other. The inside destination is set up by the diagonal view, so that on a rainy day, you'd feel quite satisfied to sit here and enjoy gazing out in both directions. But on a beautiful day, it's the place that welcomes you into the garden. Its wide windows and sturdy French sliding doors make the transition to the outside areas a gracious and satisfactory experience.

—Sarah

This home shows the importance of containing space so that different functions can happen in discrete spaces. Starting with the most obvious kind of container—a reflecting pool in which water is held in by low stone walls—you can find a host of different sizes and shapes around the house.

1	2	3
4	5	6
7	8	9

4 **5** **Containers of billowing** annuals and perennials grace the garden pool, extending the blooming season and providing focal accents. Behind the pool, bamboo, golden ray (*Ligulana x* "The Rocket") and hakonegrass (*Hakonechloa macra* "Aureola") provide a lush border.

7 **To the left** of the garage is an outdoor room (a room-size container) for basketball with a concrete half wall and white-painted pipe railings that look like a fenced terrace. The hoop peeks over the Kousa dogwood and ornamental grasses planted in front.

8 **A garden room** can be a container, too. Here, a slider opens from the sunroom onto this three-sided, fenced terrace, designed as a space for contemplation. The enclosures set this outside room apart from its surrounds while allowing it to feel linked to the life of the family when the sliders are open.

Rooms Inside and Out

Most of us seek to create a home that feels welcoming to family and friends. So many qualities come into play to make this happen. With a house like this suburban Boston residence, it's the projections that open out to engage the landscape. The little dormer windows peek out from the shingled roofline of the gambrel-style house, and the many "ells" push off into the landscape, occupying space and creating inhabitable corners—an outside version of the Not So Big principle "shelter around activity." The landscape responds to these architectural moves by pushing out and pulling back to hide and reveal a series of outdoor garden rooms.

The indoor and outdoor rooms and passageways define the essence of this home. Giant spruce trees line the driveway as an evergreen allée, allowing a sense of formal passage while creating

NOT SO BIG INSIDE OUT

Not So Big doesn't necessarily mean small. It's more about the sensibility toward space both inside and out. This beautiful home includes intimate and expansive outdoor places, all of them woven together with the house to create a veritable wonderland, and all perfectly proportioned to accompany the scale of the house. There's a simple elegance to the composition of the various elements of this garden that greatly enhances the experience of everyday living.   —*Sarah*

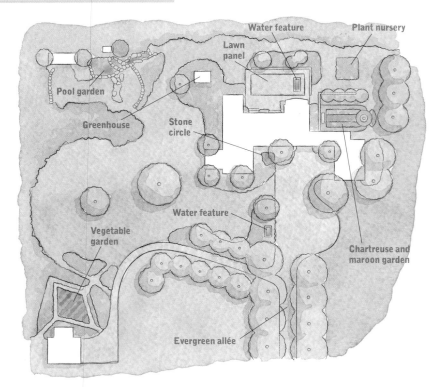

Water feature

Lawn panel

Plant nursery

Pool garden

Greenhouse

Stone circle

Water feature

Vegetable garden

Chartreuse and maroon garden

Evergreen allée

∨ Creating color echoes in your garden helps bring rhythm and harmony to its composition. This wonderful chartreuse and lime agave responds to the low-growing bamboo leaves, set off by the deep green of the clematis vine growing up a wooden trellis on the side of the house.

∧ A granite trough anchors one end of this oblong lawn. Owner and designer combined their horticultural talents to create a lushly-planted garden.

a visual and psychological barrier between house and public road. Similarly, a brick path acts as a corridor between outdoor rooms. Its planted "walls" provide linkage and screening at the same time.

A Garden Full of Rooms

Landscape designer and horticulturist Gary Koller, working closely with his client, began by developing rooms around the house. He started with a beautiful herb garden, a plant nursery, and a lawn parterre that parallels the living room to the rear; all use planted and built enclosures to wall themselves from the rooms around them. If you think of the lawn as sitting on a horizontal plane, and of the plants as occupying a vertical plane, you can see how Gary designed this space. The bluestone path defines the edge of the lawn plane, and the stunning Japanese maple, sourwood tree, and ornamental onion below fill in the palette of the vertical plane.

Bulbs soften the low, oblong stone water basin, placed on axis with the kitchen ell. So simple, it is a place that is equally effective for contemplation as for entertainment. By the driveway, a similarly shaped stone water basin—this time supported between two vertical stones—stops the eye. It is a small event along the way. A grander event—a greenhouse—draws you inside to view seedlings and tender plants that need protection through the winter months. It hides in a flurry of plantings at the end of the lawn panel. Other events include spectacular trees and unusual shrubs that provide visiting gardeners many hours of horticultural delight.

A guest cottage sits in another corner of this 4-acre parcel. The owner decided to use it as a foil for her vegetable garden. Vegetables grown in raised garden beds often do better than their counterparts on the ground. Edges unify the design, contain the soil, and make maintenance—tilling the soil, weeding, watering—easier. The surrounding gravel pathways also make gardening

∧ Both clients and designer treated every last corner of this yard as a garden. Even along the driveway—normally considered a purely functional area—they placed a water feature, an echo of the rectangular pool in the terrace garden.

∧ Every serious gardener has a plant nursery. This former vegetable garden became too shady and was turned into a place for the owner to nurture seedlings, hold plants until they are ready to be planted, or nurse them back to health.

∧ This low-growing variety of bamboo has lime-green leaves with a velvety underside.

∨ A neat brick walkway edged in cobblestones takes a visitor under a mature Japanese maple to a turn in the path. The trunks of the tree obscure the view, adding to the sense of anticipation about what lies ahead.

easier by choking out weeds while radiating the sun's warmth into the adjoining beds. As you can see on the plan, the vegetable garden sits many yards away from the house—a kind of "away garden" that allows the owner a room of her own for growing.

An Outside Away Room In *The Not So Big House*, Sarah defined an "away room" as a space in the home that allows the activities that require peace and quiet to be separated from those that generate noise. The same can be said for outside a Not So Big House. A swimming pool can be a source of noisy activity, so locating it away from quieter pursuits around the home can be helpful. Here, Gary placed the swimming pool in an upper corner of the garden. This pool garden is reached by a secret stairway of stone that follows the hillside in a series of steps and platforms. Near the top of the slope, the stepping-stones begin to meld together to create a

< Some entry points are obvious; others, like this one, are more subtle. This path up to the pool garden, constructed of large, flat fieldstones, winds through plantings and alongside a falling stream.

terrace with one long stone breaking free to cross a small pool of water lilies, iris, and red and green cut-leaf Japanese maples (*Acerpalmatum dissectum* cultivars) along its shores. At the swimming pool, the stones become steps in the water and curl around the pool as a terrace, nestled back into a ledge-strewn hillside and surrounded by trailing shrubs and perennials. A charming pool house, swathed in Japanese hydrangea vine (*Schizophragma*

> Flat fieldstones are tightly jointed to form a sitting terrace. Looser joints allow small-leafed plants like thyme (*Thymus spp.*) to spread over the stones, while the cantilevered coping becomes a set of steps into the pool itself.

> The pool garden is a special outdoor destination announced by a handsome ornamental iron gate. The irregular shape of the pool, along with the pockets of plantings that soften its edge, makes it feel like a natural pond.

> A fieldstone bridge fords the artificial stream on the way to the pool garden, just one of the many pleasures on this delightful journey.

Points of Entry

Here, a driveway is a garden, too, and it deserves the special consideration given to all parts of the landscape. Designer Gary Koller created a series of gestures that make this one an entry court. You enter under an allée of high spruce trees that screen the house from view. At the first of two parking areas, Gary created a special event: a stone water basin with a veil of water trickling over its edge, humidifying the air as it dampens the crunch of tires on gravel. You park and look for the front entrance, located at the corner created by two ells of the house. Here, the front door opens onto a circle of bluestone and cobbles surrounded by plantings that defines the point of entry into the house.

Another point of entry invites you directly into the garden. An extension of shingled wall links garage to house and acts as a gateway to the garden rooms beyond. Because there is no glass in the windows, the structure looks like the wall of the house but acts like a garden fence. A stone ramp allows a wheelbarrow access to the garden rooms beyond.　　—Julie

hydrangeiodes), offers a small shelter. Passing out of the garden through a decorative iron gate, the stones loosen up once more to become stepping-stones set in grass. The entire pool space feels like a dream landscape, hidden away yet self-sufficient.

This home shows us that you can organize a whole property as a series of garden rooms—some close to the house, others farther away. Like the rooms in your house, each outdoor room divides a large space into a series of manageable parts that can be of different sizes, uses, and styles.

Alignment

SYMMETRY CAN BE a satisfying organizational device for an outside landscape. Here, brick paths define the edges of this garden room, with rows of plantings linking foreground to background, like stripes on the earth. Flanked by birdhouses, a curved teak bench offers a secure viewing position that aligns with the house and the focal stone lantern that occupies the center of the garden space.

A sunroom window (at far right on the facing page) offers a direct line of sight onto this garden when open. Choosing plants that grow to a height just below a window jamb underlines the view. In this case, a low-growing bamboo gives color and texture to this lime-green and emerald garden. *—Julie*

HOMESCAPING

Outdoor Focus

Many traditional houses, like this one, have relatively small windows that make it difficult to really invite the outside in. These houses were designed during an era when glass was expensive, when the cold that they allowed in made the house a challenge to heat, and when direct sunlight caused fading of fabrics and rugs. There are two common solutions for today's owners of such houses who want more connection with their gardens. You can increase the size and number of windows, or you can add a room like this one (below right), devoted to appreciation of the surrounding landscape.

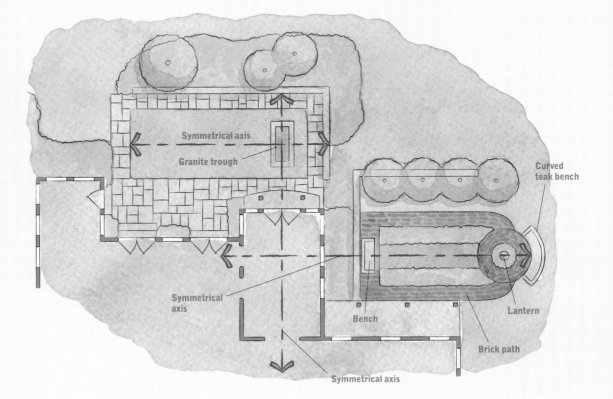

Symmetrical axis

Granite trough

Curved teak bench

Symmetrical axis

Bench

Lantern

Brick path

Symmetrical axis

In 1987, the homeowners added this sunroom to provide a comfortable place to sit that gave them the sense of being outside. In the winter, when the doors and windows are closed, the volume of the space, with its high clerestory windows, provides a light and airy embrace, or sanctuary, from the snow-covered tree limbs. In the summer, the high windows transform into a green frieze that filters direct light.

A room that has such an outdoor focus can give you the feeling that you are sitting inside a prism or crystal, looking out through the many facets into the beauty of nature. The experience is enhanced by the use of multipaned windows. The divisions in the glass create a simple pattern overlay that breaks the view into bite-size pieces. They give you a set of mini frames to see through, which, in turn, draw your attention to particular features in the landscape.

—Sarah

Alignment

WHEN A WINDOW or doorway is aligned with an important feature in the surrounding landscape, there's a powerful sense of order and balance. We can literally feel the interconnection between inner and outer worlds. Julie has described the symmetrical composition of this linear garden, but it's not until you view it from inside the sunroom that you really appreciate the full extent of the alignment. The center set of large casement windows, over 6 ft. tall, invite in the view to the garden beyond. The flanking casements align with the brick path. The effect from the sunroom is to experience the room and garden as components of a single place, part of it inside and part of it outside. *—Sarah*

and plantings—help shape our sense of home.

Details
Crafting the Elements of Nature

This unusual and sophisticated front yard, with its multitextured planting beds and yellow columns gracing the portico, reveals the hand of the landscape designer/owner, an inveterate plants person with an artistic bent.

A Garden of Earthly Delights

Landscape designer Rosalind Reed and her husband, Howard Walker, don't mind creating a stir in their neighborhood. When you drive down their street in the leafy suburb of Oak Park, Illinois, you can't miss their home: The three towering spires of arborvitae act like a verdant billboard advertising the delights of her garden's design. In the shadow of the 25-ft. trees lies a landscape of diverse plant species with multiple textures, colors, and sizes, all weaving together around the boxy gray house. With its hipped roof pulled down low over the upper windows and its portico of bright yellow columns announcing the front door, the house looks surprised and delighted at what its owners have wrought. Their immediate neighbors are particularly pleased, since Roz, as she's known, has begun helping them landscape their front yards as well.

NOT SO BIG INSIDE OUT

In planning this book, we wanted good examples of houses on Not So Big lots that still use the space to create a sequence of outdoor spaces. Here, the challenge is even greater due to the fact that there are neighbors on three sides of the property. This garden eloquently illustrates how good design can bring into being a magical and secluded universe that's completely unexpected and quite transporting in its beauty.
—*Sarah*

The clean lines of the front façade of the Reed-Walker house contrast with the large brick courtyard, whose abundant plantings blanket the front yard. Offset from the front porch is a broad brick path that seems to flow under the concrete sidewalk that parallels the street. By not aligning front walk to front door, Roz ensures that everyone who walks onto her property will stroll through the garden court, enjoying the plantings, benches, and small but effective focal points along the way. She uses planting beds to carve out space, creating a circular path of reddish gravel around an island full of a mix of annuals, perennials, and shrubs, all artfully combined to create a voluptuous whole.

The delights continue as you are beckoned around the house by a series of large stepping-stones that winds along a dry streambed. In this narrow side yard, Roz intensifies the sensory experience by closing down space. Moving underneath a limb of a magnolia tree that acts as a gateway into the tunnel-like shade, you soon realize that you've left the open, sunny experience of the front court far behind. The soothing sounds of water beckon, traveling from basin to basin. Further along lies a recirculating pond, which appears out of the dry streambed. Roz has cleverly designed a watery journey, with sounds and cooling atmospheric effects that lure you to the back garden.

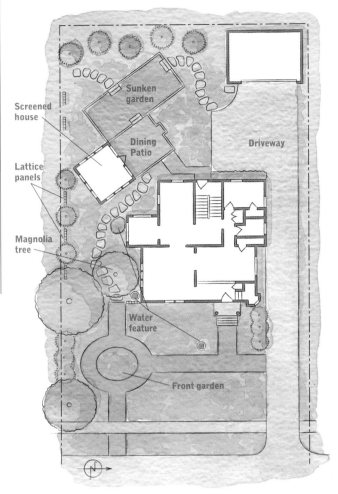

Screened house

Sunken garden

Dining Patio

Driveway

Lattice panels

Magnolia tree

Water feature

Front garden

N

V The public sidewalk crosses a brick path that turns into a circle in the front garden. This island planting breaks up the path and brings a point of interest to the space.

> Three vertical evergreen spires baffle the front porch and bring the house into scale, a treatment that is unlike any other on the block.

< When you treat your front yard as though it's your backyard, the possibilities for aesthetic and horticultural delight are endless. The landscape designer/owner contrasts a broad Japanese maple tree with four columnar pines to enclose the space and lend it intimacy.

∧ A turquoise blue pot bobs in a sea of verdant textures. By featuring different shades of green in this garden, the home-owner has an endless array of plants to choose from. A different colored pot here might ruin the harmonious effect.

Away Rooms in the Garden

Although planted down to the last square inch, the back garden is made up of a number of rooms—some big and some small; some for entertaining and some for getting away. The focal point of the backyard is a detached screened house placed on the diagonal from the main house. While built as an outdoor room for eating and entertaining, it also allows Roz and Howard a spot to quietly enjoy a glass of wine or read the paper, just a few steps from the back door of the house. When lit at night, this outdoor away room glows warmly on a summer's evening, providing shelter from inclement weather and unwelcome insects.

∧ This "dry landscape" was influenced by Japanese design, then filled with flowers. Here, the "stream" of gravel tumbles past false dragonhead and under an old magnolia tree.

∧ Who wouldn't be drawn to sit in this purple Adirondack chair? This contemplative place is carved out of beds of large-leafed hostas—an indestructible shade-tolerant plant with an astonishing number of varieties.

∨ The homeowners' backyard feels like a completely different experience from the front yard. Common and inexpensive landscape materials—concrete block, concrete brick, and red gravel—were used with flair.

While the screened room acts as fulcrum for the whole design (see p. 168), two terrace areas occupy most of the backyard. A sunken garden offers space for large numbers of people. A simple oblong filled with the same red gravel used in the front yard, it demonstrates an inexpensive way to carve out backyard space. Concrete block walls that retain the earth around the perimeter provide both seating and an edging that holds in the gravel. The upper dining patio houses a Mexican clay oven, a grill, and a table and chairs; its location just a few steps down from the kitchen makes it an easy destination. Peeking out among the lush plantings, you can also find several spots that lure you to sit and look back on this realm of sensory delights.

Vertical Screening

Roz uses tall vertical elements to provide screening, yet allow the neighbors views into her garden wherever she deems it appropriate. In the front yard, a weeping pine tree blocks direct views into the garden while creating a clear sightline to the front door. In the backyard, she employs a wonderful technique to ensure that her next-door neighbors can enjoy her garden. Three lattice panels, measuring 4 ft. wide by 6 ft. high, are spaced 5 ft. apart. In the space between panels, Roz has planted an evergreen tree that will grow high and wide enough to block direct views, yet be a living, growing divider, a welcome break from the relentless separation of a wooden fence.

∧ Roz didn't want to block her neighbors from looking into her garden, so she used latticework panels and left openings for conifer trees, which will eventually grow to fill the space.

The Beautiful Line

What is it about a curving path that so excites the mind? Think of the beauty of an oxbow of a river or the inward curving eddies in a rushing brook. Such beautiful lines form the backbone of landscape design, deriving from the geometric forms of architecture and the curvaceous lines of nature.

Such curves often stand in stark contrast to the buildings that define their edges. Within leftover rectilinear spaces, curves feel especially right to the eye. These voluptuous curves are the yin of nature that completes the yang of the architecture.

When I explain the beauty of curves to a client, I'll use orange biodegradable spray paint. I love to draw out the unfurling of a fern frond, or the inward spiraling of a path up to the top of a mount, or the location of a pinched "waist" in a walkway, like an hourglass shape on the land. As I sketch, I feel as though I am caressing the ground I walk upon, honoring it by giving it form, by offering up the most beautiful silhouette I can create. No matter what kind of garden I'm designing, finding the beautiful line is my perpetual quest.

—*Julie*

outside
| parallels |

Outdoor Room

THE COMPONENTS of an outdoor room are the same as for one that's indoors: some walls, a floor, and a ceiling. In a landscape, walls can be high or low, of hard materials or soft. In homeowner Rosalind Reed's sunken garden, masonry walls are only 15 in. high, with plants providing upper-story screening from view.

Outdoor flooring can be made of wood, stone, tile, or even grass; Rosalind chose a gravel ground cover as the floor of the sunken garden. The out-of-doors equivalent to a ceiling could be a trellis, a pergola, a garden house, an arbor, a tree canopy, or in this case, the sky itself.   —*Julie*

Implied Walls

Unlike a solid wall, which can seem like an affront to neighbors, an implied wall of plant material (see p. 167) is almost always welcomed, especially when it's an enhancement for everyone. Even when there's nothing particularly exciting to look at in a surrounding garden, the tree foliage itself provides a deeply satisfying and ever-changing tableau from the interior of the house—especially when windows are large enough to invite the outside in, as here. The delightfully shaped beech tree, which stands to the southeast of the living room, is close enough to the house that it feels like the outer wall of the room. As the sun moves across the sky during the day, the leaves, which are lit from above and behind, change in both color and light intensity, and the shadows cast by adjacent foliage modulate the color of the room itself.

A tree that's lit from behind, like this one, can be an awe-inspiring sight. Every vein of every leaf can be seen highlighted against the luminous green

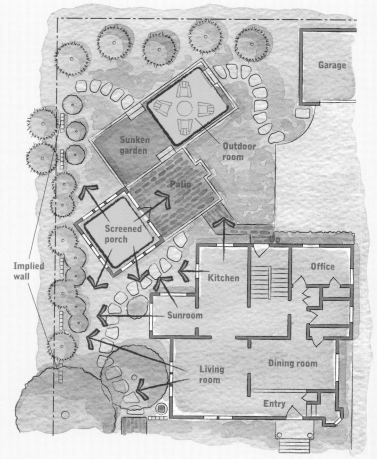

Outdoor Room

MOST PEOPLE conceive of an outdoor room as a porch, screened or not, attached to the house. If only one side is open to the elements, it hardly feels outdoors at all. Three open sides, and we really start to feel the connection with the surroundings. We are projected out into the landscape, but there's still a strong connection to the house.

The outdoor room shown here, however, is even more of an exterior space, with all four sides exposed. It's more akin to a gazebo than to an attached porch, yet it's close enough to the house to be remembered and so used daily. Just as with interior rooms, if you can't see a space, or if it's out of the way, it won't be used very often. But make it easily seen, and usage increases. —*Sarah*

of its surroundings. This may seem minor, and even trite, but to experience this up close can be the high point of each day.

On the second floor, too, the tree canopy provides the backdrop for an otherwise unremarkable view. The neighbor's house predominates from this angle, but when Rosalind sits at her drafting table, her gaze is directed to the tree. So even if you can't move windows—or trees—how you locate your furnishing with respect to the available views can make a big difference to the quality of your experience. —*Sarah*

Rosalind Reed's backyard is designed for dining and entertainment—a set of terraces that seem as if they sit in a secluded clearing in the forest, yet are surrounded on three sides by neighbors. Details are simple, inexpensive, and completely successful.

1	2	3
4	5	6
7	8	9

3 **When this hybrid rose mallow bud** opens in the sun, it will have 8-in. to 10-in. flowers. Placed in a protected location, it thrives in colder climates like Chicago.

1 **It's hard to find** well-designed outdoor lighting for a garden, but this little copper-roofed fixture is just the right size for the small-leafed creeping Jenny (*Lysimachia nummularia* "Aurea") at its feet.

6 **The Mexican clay oven** has its own place on the concrete-block retaining wall.

9 **Brick and limestone** make a handsome couple, especially when paired with purple coneflower (*Echinacea purpurea*) blossoms.

8 **One shrub that looks great** weeping over walls is called cotoneaster. Its dense, arching branches form layers where they overlap with creeping Jenny.

One of the three cabins peers out from behind a forest of Douglas firs and madrone trees, looking as if it has always been there. This one is the couple's primary living space.

Three Cabins in a Forest

Many of us long to live a simple life in a cabin in a forest, far away from the stresses and strains of the world. This couple does just that, living on a cliff above the Straits of Juan de Fuca in Port Townsend, Washington, in a self-contained village of three shingled huts set among towering Douglas fir and madrone trees. Although equal in size, each structure houses a different set of activities: One contains the living space, another accommodates a guesthouse and office, and the last structure holds an artist studio over a garage. The first two sit at right angles to one another, enclosing a woodland garden, while the third angles outward to allow space for a lap pool and terrace. Merging the enchantment of forest, high bluff, and distant views, the site is further enhanced by gardens, water features, and six bald eagles that nest in nearby trees.

NOT SO BIG INSIDE OUT

Some properties are large and ranging, while the houses upon them are small and personable. These sites present a challenge for their homeowners, who have to decide how much of the territory they are going to manicure and develop, and how much to leave in its natural state. This home finds a wonderful balance between the two, and the three structures that collectively form the house define exterior places and pathways at the heart of the site. —*Sarah*

∧ The entry porch floats above the forest floor, its supporting posts nearly indistinguishable from the tree trunks beyond. Forming the link between the residence and the guesthouse, this roofed aerial platform offers a place to choose your destination.

∨ From the guest parking lot, a reverse-curve path offers the first indication of how to move through the forest to reach the house.

When approaching the property, visitors turn up a path, which, like a bend in a road, piques their curiosity about what's up ahead. The lane winds through the trees, leading them to a small parking lot where a stone path beckons. Framed by redbud trees, the path funnels guests up a hill toward the house, catching a glimpse of its roof ahead in the trees. Path lights are twinkling guideposts at night.

The long wood and metal bridge allows visitors to fully experience being in the forest. The diagonal lines of the madrone trees—an orange-barked native of California—interrupt the vertical trunks of the Douglas fir, the signature tree of America's scenic Northwest. The varied topography of the land naturally creates a variety of outdoor spaces, with more than half of the site's seven acres remaining in its natural state. Visitors walk a distance of 200 ft. with a grade change of more than 40 ft. from guest parking to entrance level.

At the end of a long wooden staircase, an entry porch seems to float above the forest floor, its supporting posts nearly indistinguishable from the tree trunks beyond. Forming the link between the residence on the left and the guesthouse on the right, this roofed aerial platform offers a place to choose one's destination.

< Metalwork is used as a subtle thematic idea throughout the property. The fence railings relate to the metal hinges, joinery, downspouts, fountain, fire bowl, and metal roofs, all of which bear a similar color and patina.

∧ A long bridge leads visitors to a steep stairway that reaches the roofed entry porch joining two of the cabins. Orange-barked madrone trees lean across the end of the bridge, reaching up to find sunlight above the tree trunks.

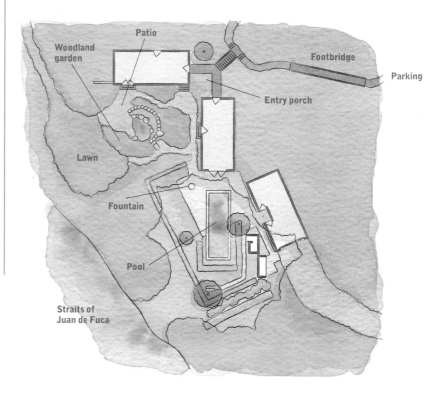

Patio

Woodland garden

Footbridge

Parking

Entry porch

Lawn

Fountain

Pool

Straits of Juan de Fuca

∨ At the edge of the property, erosion has torn trees from their roots to create a dramatic view of the straits.

> Beneath the bay window, a beam seems to pass through the post, connecting inside to outside. We are drawn to places where such boundaries are blurred, for they help us visually link our houses to their surroundings.

∧ On a large site like this, it looks best to shape planting-bed edges in sweeping curves with attention to the quality of the line between grass and plantings.

Wandering through the garden, you arrive at the very edge of the world: a sheer drop to the Straits of Juan de Fuca hundreds of feet below. High vantages with steep drops alternately repel us out of fear and draw us outward to the view. Here, overcoming our trepidation is worthwhile: Sailboats, barges, and steamers glide past islands across the straits.

The Woodland Garden

This landscape is a place of soft layers that filter sunlight onto the forest floor below. The residence

∧ Two species of shrubs intertwine wonderfully to form soft hillocks in the landscape (*Hebe* "Red edge" and *Alchemilla ellenbeckii*) are pruned together with shears to create these billowing shapes, so effective at the base of tall trees.

∨ A small stone pool is fed by a central bronze water feature, sculpted by a local artist. Echoing the forms of adjacent tree trunks, it also offers a moist atmosphere and gentle sounds to this sylvan place.

Softening Hardness

One of the things I love most about working in the landscape is that there are so many ways to soften something that is hard. What is hard in a garden? Buildings, terraces, decks, arbors, walls, fences, and paths are elements whose solidity, rigidity, linearity, or stiff nature tends to look better with something softening their edges. Usually, plants can do the trick. Climbers can soften vertical elements, cascading forms can weep over containers that sit on decks and terraces, and ground covers can grow over the edges of driveways and fences. Plantings that grow up from the ground or down from the planting bed can soften the hardness of a wall. Rather than demolishing these curved cobble retaining walls, the landscape architect chose to leave some, build steps and terraces next to others, and bury some with soil and plantings. Using the many forms of plants to soften hardness helps inter- weave the elements that make up the landscape of home.

—Julie

> The owners thought carefully about matching the color of landscape elements to the building's trim color. Here, a soft mauve paint on the window mullions is echoed in the large clay vessel that stands as a focal point on the bluestone terrace.

and guesthouse form a sheltering corner for a garden that flourishes beneath the forest canopy. The horizontal branching structure of the Japanese maple trees adds a middle story between the high fir trees overhead and the billowing shrubs at their feet. Different colors and textures weave together into soft mounds that contrast with the fissured trunks of the Douglas firs. By planting species with similar growth habits in odd-numbered groupings, a sense of continuity is created.

On most properties, contractors clear away all the trees around a house, but not here. Instead, trees grow right up to the walls, and clearings are few and far between. Light descends in long shafts through the tall trunks to highlight details such as the central fountain with its trunklike metal water rod or the pools of light that dapple across the long lines of lawn.

< Sharply angled beds of hair grass (*Nasella tenuissima*) and native evergreen huckleberries (*Vaccinium ovatum*) stand out against the more natural forest floor beyond. The delicate texture of the grasses also contrasts effectively with the bluestone that edges the pool.

< This huge, faceted vessel is made of Lunastone, a fired clay that can stand up to freezing and thawing in colder climates. Behind, palmetto trees screen a small building and stand in stark contrast to the Douglas firs beyond.

∧ The atmospheric delights of a heated swimming pool combined with scented plants, the sounds of birds, and the thermal delight of this fire bowl offer an enticement to enjoy the twilight out of doors and late into the evening.

< Plants like this Lenten rose (*Hellebore sp.*), with chartreuse leaves and mauve flowers, were selected to echo the color theme around the pool.

outside
parallels

Reflecting the Sky

A FORESTED SPACE can feel dark if there is no sense of sky. To heighten the sky's presence, find a way to recline in the landscape, with a chaise lounge or deck chairs like these that allow you to look up through the trees. Another way is to bring the sky down into your plane by reflecting it on a continuous smooth surface. Here, the unmullioned windows bring the changing colors of sky, clouds, and treetops directly into the garden. Similarly, a reflecting surface on the ground, such as a pool, pond, or polished dark stone, can mirror the sky, bringing it down to your level. Finally, find or develop an edge condition, where you can get out from under the tree canopy and look out onto a wide expanse, directly into the sky.　　　　*—Julie*

Shelter Around Activity

We are physiologically programmed to seek out places that offer a modicum of protection, particularly for our backs, so that we feel less vulnerable and more comfortable. It's why we tend to seek out a corner seat in a public place or restaurant, and the principle is just as applicable for outside spaces as inside. Readers familiar with my work know that I refer to this as "shelter around activity."

In this beautiful but rambling property, the architect and landscape architect have collaborated to create outdoor spaces that give the homeowners a sense of shelter. By breaking the house into three separate structures and locating them at angles to one another, corners have been made. Although these corners are outside spaces, they still have the characteristics that make all corners so appealing. In each case, two surrounding walls provide protection, but there's also a wide-open view to the surrounding landscape on the other two sides. In the corner made by the house and office structures, the landscape architect, Linda Attaway, has crafted a comfortable sitting area adjacent to a small pond, which in turn is circumscribed by a semicircular stone wall.

Another corner, this one created by the short end of the office and the wide side of the garage/studio, shelters the pool in much the same way. Low hedges on both sides offer a little more protection without obstructing views to the cliff edge and ocean beyond.

When you are planning the layout of a larger piece of land like this from scratch, you can use the forms of buildings to help shape and give shelter to outdoor spaces. Even if the house is a single structure, by including a wing or even a bump-out you can help create this sense of shelter around activity, which will make the outdoor sitting places more comfortable to sit in and more frequently used.

—Sarah

Reflecting the Outside

ONE OF THE most effective ways to blur the distinction between inside and outside is to continue the materials used on the interior of the house through to the exterior, while simultaneously minimizing the frames around windows and the points at which they meet these continuous

surfaces. In the main living area, you can see just how effective this strategy can be. You could easily believe that this is a screened porch rather than an air-conditioned room. The illusion is created by the extension of beams and ceiling materials beyond the boundary created by the windows below. Instead of using standard opening windows, the architect used fixed double-pane, nonoperable glass panels, so there's no need for screens or window sashes. *—Sarah*

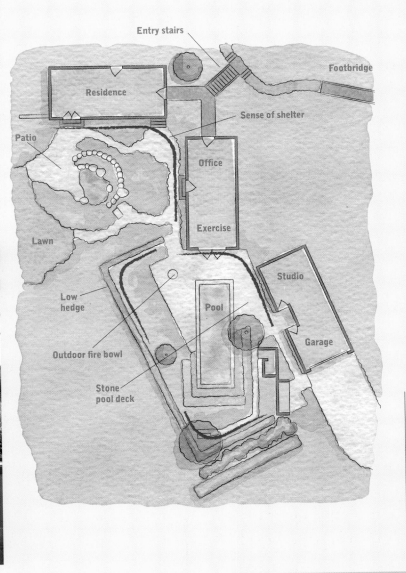

Entry stairs

Footbridge

Residence

Sense of shelter

Patio

Office

Lawn

Exercise

Low hedge

Studio

Pool

Outdoor fire bowl

Garage

Stone pool deck

Outdoor spaces like this patio, with a chunky stone fireplace and rustic posts, make use of local materials and signal the western style of this mountain ranch.

At Home on the Range

D on't we all long to own a remote hut nestled into a hillside that looks across a vast expanse to distant mountaintops, far away from the madding crowd? The Old Snowmass Ranch in Aspen, Colorado, satisfies the need for vantage and vista while providing the comfort of snuggling into a hillside on the site of an old ranch. A *feng shui* practitioner would find this setting perfect: The house faces south, backed up by higher ground that protects it, with surface water that drains into the wide valley below. Across the way, you can see all the way to the Snowmass Wilderness Area in a wide panoramic view.

The house, designed by architect Larry Yaw for an active couple whose children were grown, was consciously located at the junction between pastureland and the hillside above. Building on this theme, landscape architect Richard Shaw chose to control the views

NOT SO BIG INSIDE OUT

A number of houses in this book borrow from their neighbor's landscapes, but this house, located in an expansive meadow in the Colorado Rocky Mountains, gives borrowing the landscape new meaning. Designed to look and feel like a small cluster of cottages, the ranch, with its layers of garden, trees, and wildflowered meadows, provides a foreground for the dramatic surrounding mountain views. —*Sarah*

∨ A path of local flat fieldstone wends its way from front door to garage. Hydrangeas, perennial geranium, and sweet woodruff drift in layers at the feet of native aspen trees.

Hot tub

Deck

Deck

Terrace

Entry garden

Hedgerow

Vegetable garden

N

by hiding and revealing the magnificent vistas at different parts of the site. On the east, he planted cottonwood trees in rows that replicate traditional agricultural windscreens and protect the house and site from the strong winds that sweep across the valley. These trees allow him to edit the views to either side of the house, framing the panorama to the south.

Arriving from the circular driveway, visitors enter the house by traveling along a winding stone path through a lush perennial garden, located in a courtyard between the garage and the main wing of the house. On a side path to the garage, aspen trees, from the same family as the cottonwoods, provide shade and screening. In this intimate garden setting, Richard offers no hint of the vistas to come, hiding the climax of the experience from view. Only after

> To get to the front door, visitors meander through a delicious tangle of flowers and foliage, planted with low perennials near the path and vertical ones near the buildings. It feels like walking through a river valley.

walking through the house and coming out onto the south-facing terrace is the mountain scene revealed.

Transitional Spaces

The terrace sits in a sun pocket protected from the western winds by the bedroom wing of the house. Here, a bent gambel-oak post supports a sunscreen structure that acts like a porch off the house, complete with glider and rockers. With corrugated fiberglass panels creating the roof, this wooden structure provides shade through the heat of the day and protection from inclement weather. Such a transitional area—the space

∧ Lines that bisect the view into foreground, middle ground, and background landscapes help flatten or carve out space. Here, the foreground is the belt of aspen trees; the middle ground is the more distant hedgerow; and the background is the mountain ridgeline.

∧ The gambel-oak post dances at the edge of the porch, where it holds up a corrugated fiberglass-covered trellis structure that lends shade to this space between house and landscape.

∧ The homeowners wanted their house to reflect their informal lifestyle. Different places to be outside offer a range of experiences: a picnic table for group dining, a pair of rocking chairs and a glider for quiet conversation, and a hot tub for soaking under the stars.

∧ Imagine removing the aspen trees at the edge of this terrace and you'd create a completely different spatial experience. Besides bringing needed shade to this outdoor living room, the trees define and enclose it.

between the house and the land—invites a different kind of use than is possible when you sit inside or out. The slight vantage of one foot above the stone terrace enables you to gaze out over the land. Having the wall of the house at your back and the structure overhead, you feel protected. Located adjacent to the living room, this is a natural outdoor extension of the room.

Two steps down bring you to a stone terrace, where a simple wooden picnic table invites alfresco dining and informal entertaining. At night, the homeowners enjoy access to an outdoor fireplace and a stone-sided hot tub for warmth in the cool summer evenings. The whole is contained by a stone sitting wall that acts like a balcony or parapet, meant to protect you from a steep or dangerous drop. Beyond the wall is a lovely swath of lawn that leads to a wildflower meadow where pasture used to be. When you add in the magnificent views, this outdoor living space creates a protected and comfortable vantage for contemplating the larger landscape.

Another outdoor space is connected to the main terrace by a stepping-stone path and sits directly outside of the country kitchen and the dining room with its built-in window seat. Here, a small breakfast terrace is screened from the road by conifer trees and a pruned hedge, under the shade of a white canvas umbrella that matches the color of the clouds. Just off the master bedroom, you can enjoy yet another vantage point: a deck to take in the view under the protection of the wooden roof. From inside the house, the majestic views continue.

∧ Red, white, and pink Sweet William seed themselves with abandon in the wildflower meadow.

> With such a broad panorama as this out the back door, it's important to establish a sense of definition and rootedness for those taking in the view. Here at the breakfast terrace, low hedges surround the teak table and chairs, bringing intimacy to an otherwise immense space.

A Village on the Land

The Old Snowmass Ranch was designed to look like a little village or a compound of separate buildings that happen to share the same walls. By using different materials to clad the house, the architect creates the illusion of a house broken down into different but related parts. The main house, with its clerestory windows, board-and-batten siding, and stone foundation connected to massive stone fireplaces, contrasts wonderfully with the barnlike bedroom wing that juts out into the landscape toward the south. A red tin roof defines the main structure, while hardy asphalt shingles roof the wings. Using traditional materials to break down spaces into smaller but integral pieces, Old Snowmass Ranch carries off a deft balancing act of scale, wedding it beautifully to the mountains that surround it.

< When you look at the number of different rooflines that make up this Colorado ranch, you get the sense that it has been added onto as needed over time. The layout feels random and the materials eclectic, yet together they balance the composition.

∧ The perfect vantage: a comfortable armchair that sits on a private roofed porch set just above the treetops. From here, visitors look out to a distant view—alone.

A Space for Gardening

Nothing beats the pleasure of harvesting your own vegetables and growing flowers for your own table. This garden is given a prime southerly location, which is the best orientation for growing full-sun plants like vegetables. Layers of compost—kitchen waste, grass clippings, and leaf cuttings—have been combined to make a soil that is rich in nutrients.

Surrounded by beds of daylilies, poppies, and other perennials, it's the fence that most pleases the eye here. Made of

gambel-oak boughs, it captures the look of an old homestead in the mountains. Keeping out errant wildlife, it brings the architecture of the house out into the garden.

—*Julie*

outside
parallels

Natural Materials

ONE OF THE REASONS that the Old Snowmass Ranch appealed to us is because it uses local materials throughout to unite house to landscape. The outdoor fireplace with its massive chimney is rendered of local stone, as is the stone terrace underfoot.

The gambel oak of the posts and beams and the garden gateway are made from trees that were cleared

from the site in building the house. There's a pride attached to using natural materials straight off the property, for they add to the rustic charm of the place and further connect house and landscape to the mountains.   —*Julie*

Designing for the Way We Really Live

As we age, our objectives for our home life change as well. Instead of lives oriented around children, those with grown children, like the owners of this home, often want a feeling of peace and tranquility. The serenity of the majestic mountain views, along with the deep connection with the land that comes from cultivating both food and flowers, transforms the experience of life and provides a well-grounded foundation for these owners. They have no interest in formal rooms, preferring a house where every space is used every day.

Master bedroom

Exterior place with ceiling

Interior place with views

Pool room

Outside place

Living room

Dining room

Entry foyer

Kitchen

Interior place surrounded by view

Shelter created by building shape

Path to vegetable garden

Recognizing that they were designing this house primarily for themselves, the homeowners asked their architects to make the kitchen into the social hub, with the dining and living areas suitable for everyday use as well as entertaining. The architect and landscape designer worked to create strong interconnections between inside and out. From the kitchen, you can step outside and stroll to the vegetable garden to gather the makings for lunch. From the screen door just off the living room, you can walk out onto the covered deck that runs between dining room and bedroom wing. You can sit here and enjoy the near and distant views, or you can continue out onto the stone terrace, sheltered by the L-shaped crook created by the master bedroom wing and covered deck (see the photo on p. 182). In combination, inside and outside activity areas weave seamlessly together to give the homeowners a rich variety of places to sit and enjoy their incredible surroundings.

—Sarah

(see the photo on p. 182)

inside
parallels

Natural Materials

WHEN USED INSIDE the house, natural materials can give an organic, timeless, and permanent feel to a space. Here, the side wall of the massive living-room fireplace juts out a little into the master-bedroom hallway, its stones splayed at the base to accentuate the sense of solidity. Because we are so familiar with images of ancient structures and castles that have lasted through the centuries, stone in particular connotes agelessness.

The architects have enhanced this sense with the use of double doors made of heavy, rustic wood. Natural materials tie us to our ancestral and historical roots and give us a sense both of security and connection with the natural world around us.

—Sarah

Ovals, like this lawn panel, soothe the soul. A grass terrace in the front yard serves as a clean base for house and garden. Stone steps bisect the space and line up perfectly with the large evergreen tree in the neighbor's yard next door.

Terraces of Grass

Symmetry can be downright boring if not detailed with care. When you compose a symmetrical landscape, the resulting design is usually restful to the eye. But it can also be too obvious, too easy for the eye to take in at a glance. Owners Scott and Norma Shannon found ways to make perfect balance seem dynamic through crafted details in the artful gardens around their 2,000-sq.-ft. house in Cazenovia, New York.

The barnlike proportions and rigid symmetry of their Dutch colonial home forced the couple to choose simple geometric forms as organizing landscape elements. In the front yard, rather than resorting to foundation plantings like the rhododendron and juniper bushes found in many suburbs around the country, they chose to create a horizontal platform retained by a low stone wall that acts as a base for the house. Centered on the front façade of

NOT SO BIG INSIDE OUT

The Dutch colonial home shown here is familiar to many inner-ring suburbs. We selected this example because of the elegant but approachable formality of the garden's design on a lot that's pretty typical of neighborhoods established at the turn of the last century. Provisions for the automobile have been integrated in an innovative way, and there's a wonderful collaboration with the neighbors to give an expanded sense of the property's boundaries. —Sarah

the house is an oval of grass edged by bluestone pavers, which they call "the ellipse." This lawn panel gives form to the front yard, creating an outdoor room that acts as play space and garden. Lush plantings that spill onto the sidewalk offer a certain degree of privacy yet invite passersby to look in.

This symmetrical front yard feels dynamic because the main entry to the house is on the east side. A porch is located at the center of this façade, accessed by the narrow driveway that runs along the house. When seen from the street, the symmetrical house actually sits asymmetrically on the property, energizing the otherwise perfect balance of the grass oval and making the whole feel dynamic. Scott, a landscape architect, and Norma, an experienced gardener, used the wall to provide a clear transition from the public realm of the street to the semipublic front garden.

∧ This side garden path meanders through a delightful thicket of native shade-loving perennials. Owned by the neighbors but gardened by Scott and Norma, this path links backyards and highlights the friendly relationship between the two families.

ALL AROUND THE HOUSE

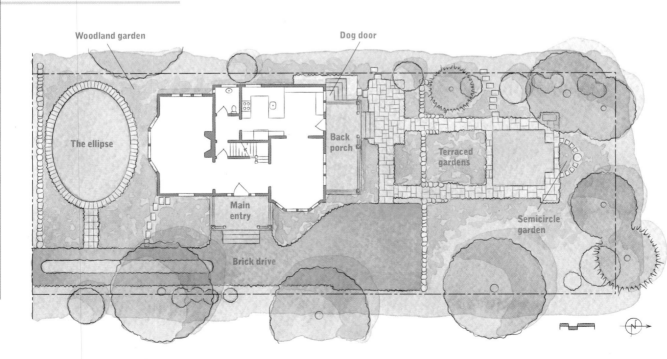

Woodland garden

Dog door

The ellipse

Main entry

Back porch

Terraced gardens

Semicircle garden

Brick drive

∧ The couple's lawn oval echoes the grass turf of the public park across the street. Shade-loving perennials, such as lady's mantle and different varieties of hostas and ferns, interweave to form a verdant tapestry.

< The tire tracks end at the side porch, which is the main entry point into the house. Notice how the brick drive cuts back to become a foundation for the wooden steps. This careful attention to detail is what makes the property so special.

∧ Windows over the porch and the three columns under it are set so that they are centered on the roof peak. Underneath the porch roof, the kitchen door and right-hand edge of the kitchen window grouping is also centered on the peak to achieve dynamic balance.

∨ Two kinds of stones—granite and flat fieldstone—interlock as elegantly as a dovetail joint. Creating such a seamless union between two materials brings a high level of refinement to the design of a garden.

Gardening on the Side
The driveway itself is as carefully crafted as the ellipse. Surfaced in red brick pavers, it doubles as a path to the front porch. A grass strip—detailed with brick edging to form an elongated oval—runs down the center of the driveway. At the end of the drive, a bricked parking court is large enough to accommodate two cars at the back of the lot. With the attention Scott has given to proportion and detail, this driveway becomes a garden.

< This terrace garden of grasses and blooms is retained by a handsome stone wall. Another oblong terrace of bluestone links the porch, garden, and dog-run steps. Such panels act like a simple pool of space, a restful backdrop to the vibrant planting beds.

The garden on the west side of the house is overflowing with plants. Sandwiched between two houses and only 10 ft. wide, this naturalized woodland garden has a moist and shady microclimate. What surprises is that the neighbors, who own most of it, happily give the couple carte blanche to design and install a shared garden that benefits both properties.

A Line of Axis

Scott and Norma decided that they wanted a stronger interior-exterior connection at the back of the house. As part of their renovation, they designed a hallway that links the pantry and kitchen areas to the breakfast nook, creating a line of axis—a path or direction of movement along a straight line—that includes the new back porch and steps and turns into a garden path. This bluestone walkway is one of two that edge the set of terraces climbing a gentle slope in the back garden. The lowest terrace is filled with flowers; one step up brings you to a terrace of grass with benches to either side. Crowned with a semicircular planting bed that has a birdbath at its center, this handsome design feels symmetrical, balanced, and perfectly proportioned for the house. Yet, because the line of axis is off center, the whole becomes dynamic.

Events Along the Way

While the layout and design of this landscape work so well to organize space, it would not be as good a garden without the many small "events." These landmarks give pause to the flow of movement along a garden path and evoke contemplation.

Some events are tiny footnotes, like the birdbath the couple used to call attention to a step along the brick walkway. Other events stand as stronger focal points, like the standing birdbath that occupies the apex of the garden. Events should pique your interest as you make your way through the garden.

—Julie

outside
| parallels |

Lining Things Up

WHY DOES IT FEEL so satisfying to line up elements outside your house? Perhaps it is because without a means of orientation, a landscape can feel overwhelmingly open and/or exposed. Making a linear relationship between house and garden serves to anchor what's outside to that which is within.

A second reason is that an axial path centered on an interior space like

a hallway brings the inside out and the outside in. Here, lining up the kitchen axis with one of the two paths that edge the borders of the symmetrical garden gives a sense of balance to the two, despite the fact that the whole is not actually centered on the house.

—Julie

Symmetry

There are a few notable alignments clearly visible on the floor plan that were part of the original house and that colored the approach that Scott and Norma took to the garden's layout. Notice first the alignment of the bay window in the dining room with the sliding doors into the kitchen. These two elements are not only aligned, they are also symmetrical about the central axis. The same is true of the bay window on the front of the house and the fireplace in the living room. In fact, if we look at the house from the street, we see that the bay window, in turn, is perfectly centered on the gable of the roof above. Had the windows on the second floor been placed asymmetrically on the front façade, the house would have a very off-kilter look.

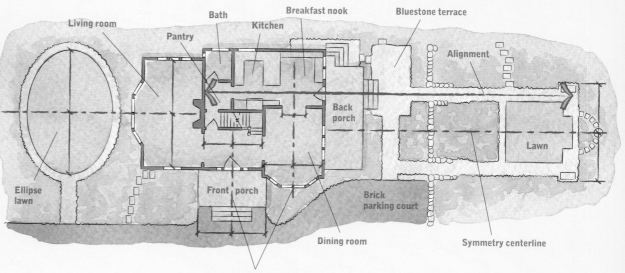

Living room · Pantry · Bath · Kitchen · Breakfast nook · Bluestone terrace · Alignment · Back porch · Lawn · Ellipse lawn · Front porch · Brick parking court · Dining room · Symmetry centerline · Symmetry centerline

Lining Things Up

OUR EYES appreciate alignment. When things are lined up, we sense that there is harmony and balance. It's as though subliminally we know that someone thought about the arrangement of spaces, objects, or views, and that we are being well taken care of.

Just the glimpse through the open kitchen door to the garden path beyond, perfectly aligned with the direction of our movement from inside to out, gives you a feeling of order as well as an invitation to explore the world beyond the walls of the house. Looking at the floor plan, you'll see that the view from the far end of the pantry also aligns with the door and path.   *—Sarah*

So when it came to designing a garden to surround the house, the possibility existed to include some symmetrical aspects within a necessarily asymmetrical design, just like the house itself. Julie has described the delightful elliptical lawn, which has been used in lieu of the typical green carpet. But it's not just an arbitrarily located ellipse. It, like the fireplace inside and the living-room bay, is exactly aligned with the ridge of the gabled roof above.

When considering the design of your own landscape, take note of the characteristics that give the house its personality and allow this to inform what you do with its surroundings. Borrowing an attitude, as here with the use of occasional symmetry, the entire composition will be more recognizably one thing, one place, one home.

—Sarah

The backyard terrace is a study in how to craft landscape details. Using symmetry as an organizing device, homeowner Scott Shannon laid out two levels, with a perennial garden in the foreground and a lawn panel behind set two steps up. At the back of the garden, he created a semicircular path with a birdbath as the central focus.

1	2	3
4	5	6
7	8	9

2 **Developing the corner** of a symmetrical garden helps stop the eye while creating a contemplative destination. Here, teak benches flank the semicircle at the end of the grass panel.

3 **6** **Paths and place intersect** at a rectangle of bluestone that serves as a threshold for a teak bench and an indentation in the grass panel. Small "events," in this case two pots and a birdbath, allow the eye to pause, while a neighbor's garage peeks out behind a vine-clad fence.

9 **Yellow sundrops** (*Oenothera tetragona*) and magenta meadowsweet (*Filipendula palmata*) bring zest to the perennial bed in June. You can play with plant combinations by trying them out. The beauty of most perennials is that if you don't like the effect, you can always move them around next year.

The vibrant cottage garden makes this delightfully crafted property sing. Light blue spires of delphinium rise out of drifts of lady's mantle, catmint, and iris foliage.

A Cottage in the City

In 1988, David and Sukie Amory—he an architect, she a gardener—returned to Boston with their two young children to open a design practice. They bought a small, boxy house in the suburb of Brookline. Like many old homes, this one had its pluses and minuses. The virtues were clear: close proximity to the city, public transportation, a 10-acre park nearby, and a wonderful silver birch tree shading the backyard. The deficits were equally obvious: squat proportions, small dark rooms, pink and green concrete pavers. The Amorys assumed they would be comfortable in the house for only a few short years. Seventeen years and several renovation projects later, the couple, with children now in college, still lives here. In a row of carefully tended lawns surrounded by chain-link fences, the Amory residence stands out as a potpourri of flowers surrounding a charming cottage.

NOT SO BIG INSIDE OUT

Frequently, with small homes in inner-ring suburbs, neither the interior nor the garden is much to look at. But this tidy little home is a testament to the fact that this doesn't have to be the case. A little attention to craft and detail can transform an average piece of property into a very beautiful and inspiring place to live. Both of us love the simplicity and attainability of this unassuming yet delightful home.

—*Sarah*

∧ Modest houses nestle close in this quiet neighborhood near Boston. Every square inch of this property is planted with flowers and foliage—but no lawn—to cut for the table all year round.

Cottage Gardens

Visitors open the wooden slatted gate, painted to match the trim on the house, and are immersed in a garden of plants of all types and colors and textures. Planted in the manner of a traditional English cottage garden, it consists of a seemingly casual mixture of flowering perennials, annuals, and shrubs that border the path to the front door, adorned with clematis and honeysuckle vines. And like a cottage garden, the whole is enclosed by a low picket fence, within which a changing tapestry of bulbs, herbs, grasses, ferns, and flowers weave together to wondrous effect.

Each season, Sukie's cottage garden enjoys a slightly different palette of blooms. The peak moment for color comes in midsummer, when soft blues, purples, and shell pinks are enlivened by touches of chartreuse, pale yellow, and vibrant red. In midsummer, green foliage sets off hues of blue and yellow. In fall, the subtle foliage is accented by garnet tones of sedum and the deep blue of monkshood.

Using Every Square Inch

Sukie has gardened every square inch in her 4,000-sq.-ft. space around the house. Along the side of the house, facing southeast, she planted a garden devoted to "old" and David Austin roses that climb within a low hedging of lavender plantings. Sukie's husband David designed a wooden pergola above the garage doors that echoes the form of the rafter tails that ornament windows facing the driveway and provides a structure for a climbing clematis vine.

∧ This spectacular Persian onion is a bulb that produces 8-in. to 10-in. blossoms with half-inch silver-coated starlike florets and dried seed heads.

<　The shade garden offers a cool, contemplative spot. Two sets of chairs enjoy different views: The twig chairs sit against the back of the house, borrowing the view of the neighbor's backyard; the bucket chairs, supported by the birch tree and garage, occupy the center of the garden space.

∨ Rafter tails act as supports for the homeowners' many varieties of climbing vines that adorn the house. Here, old-fashioned scented roses bordered by a row of lavender grow between house and driveway.

<　Maintaining clean-edged beds where the occasional plant spills over creates a pleasing informality. Here, yellow yarrow, purple-blue catmint, and lime-green lady's mantle blur the garden path.

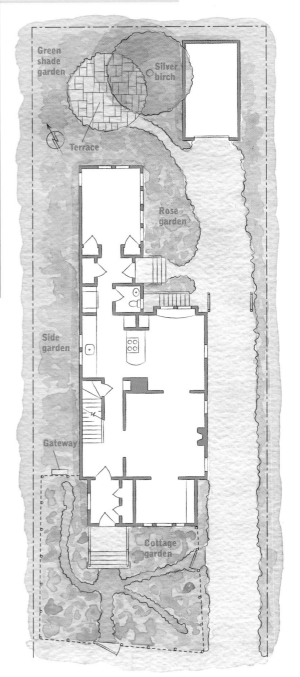

∧ Astilbe flowers of various hues brighten the narrow side yard. In the background, honeysuckle tangles over a wooden trellis while creamy lacecap hydrangea blossoms grow tall against the picket fence.

< In the Amory's shade garden, different hues and textures of green foliage combine to bring a sense of remove on a summer's day. Fern, hydrangea, ivy, and sweet woodruff foliage stand out against the darker hues of boxwood and holly.

The Relief of Shade

Inspiration for a garden's design can come from many sources. In her garden, Sukie referenced British poet Andrew Marvell's lines, "Annihilating all that's made/To a green thought in a green shade," by selecting evergreens and ground cover to set off the magnificent silver birch that shades the back of the property. Boxwood, holly, ferns, and English ivy—all shade-loving favorites—provide a verdant setting for daffodils and Spanish bluebells in the spring. Akebia, clematis, and Virginia creeper vines twine their way up the back corner of the house. (The old saying "clematis place their heads in the sun and their feet in the cool shade" is a good rule of thumb, since most species resent hot weather.)

To give form to her plantings, Sukie created two circular bluestone terraces: one nestled against the house and a larger one that occupies the middle of the small backyard space, both crowned with comfortable places to sit for an intimate couple. In order to make the small backyard feel bigger than it really is, Sukie chose to capture views through to the neighbor's extensive garden of yews, mountain laurel, and rhododendron by keeping plantings low along the back property line. Along the side, she also layered plantings of trees, shrubs, and perennials to create a sense of depth.

> Homeowner Sukie Amory trained rose and clematis vines to grow up against the front corner of her house to further connect the structure to the garden.

Dynamic Balance

Unless it's a highly ordered or perfectly symmetrical garden layout, I like to set objects in my landscape designs so that they feel balanced and dynamic. Owner Sukie Amory achieved this by scribing a circle of bluestone pavers in her shade garden, then setting a pair of bucket chairs on one side of the circle opposite a group of four pots of plants. Notice that three of the four are planted with the same boxwood shrub; the fourth, housing a topiary planting of variegated ivy leaves, forms a triangle in space with the two chairs. The whole composition feels ordered yet dynamic. In the planting bed behind the terrace, Sukie placed a birdbath on axis with the house and added Japanese painted fern in seemingly random order to add a dynamic element to the whole.

Inside the house, she used this dynamic balance with lamps, pots of plants, paintings, and furniture placed in interesting relationship to each other. Here, three windows provide a background framework that is balanced for a dynamic placement of vertical objects: two topiary standards and four white pendant floor lamps. This interior design, like its outside counterpart, will never seem predictable nor static. *—Julie*

Framed Openings

AT THE CORNER of the house by the side yard stands a metal archway covered in honeysuckle. This gateway illustrates what I call the "mouse hole" effect. Moving along the side garden, visitors notice the framed opening ahead, which narrows down and focuses their experience of the space beyond to one small, defined view.

From this dark mouse hole, you enter into the brightness of the garden filled with blossoms. Framing an opening in the landscape allows you to narrow down or decrease the scope of the space before you explode forth into a new garden realm.　　*—Julie*

Transforming Small and Outdated into Not So Big

Many older homes present a challenge for modern homeowners in that the front part of the house, where 100 years ago most of the living occurred, is completely separated from the back part, where the kitchen and utility areas reside. This work area was often the territory of the hired help, but today it's where we tend to do most of our living. Many of these older homes are left with their original floor plans more or less intact, with most of the daily activities crowded into a tiny kitchen with one small window to the back or side yard.

In this 1920s-era home, which exhibited most of these problems, the owners implemented several simple strategies to make it more livable for today, as well as to connect the inside to the lovely surrounding gardens.

The most important was the addition of an arched opening between the original kitchen and the formal dining room. By making a wide connecting view between the two, the kitchen and dining room became defined parts of one larger space. The dining room now serves as both an informal, everyday

Garden study

Bath

Kitchen

Dining

eating area and, when guests are over for dinner, a formal room.

Because the original dining room was designed for the visual pleasure of the primary inhabitants, there's much more connection to the outside from this space than from utility areas—a connection that can now be shared by the kitchen.

—Sarah

Framed Openings

IN THE FIRST part of the 20th century, framed openings were used frequently as spatial devices to differentiate one room from another, without blocking the view too much between them. The framed opening shown here is trimmed with the same woodwork as a doorway, yet its added width makes it feel very different.

While a doorway 30 in. to 36 in. wide tends to focus your attention on the small area you can see beyond, the wider framed opening becomes literally a frame for the entirety of the activity place beyond, sending a message of invitation. It welcomes you in, but it clearly delineates this place from the one you currently occupy.

—Sarah

Architects & Landscape Designers

Playing Up the Corners

CYNTHIA KNAUF LANDSCAPE DESIGN, INC.
Landscape Designer: Cynthia Knauf
138 Main St.
Montpelier, VT 05602
802.223.6447
www.cynthisknauf.com

SUSANKA STUDIOS
Architect: Sarah Susanka, FAIA
(done while at Mulfinger, Susanka, Mahady
& Partners)
www.susanka.com

Borrowing the Landscape

HENNING/ANDERSON
Landscape Architects: Heather Anderson,
Matthew Henning, ASLA
4030 Everett Ave.
Oakland, CA 94602
510.531.3095
www.henning-anderson.com

FOX DESIGN GROUP ARCHITECTS
Architect: Dennis Fox
116 Washington Ave., Suite D
Point Richmond, CA 94801
510.235.3369
www.foxdesigngroup.com

The Attraction of Opposites

JUDY HARMON, LANDSCAPE ARCHITECT
Landscape Architect: Judy Harmon
706 Mountford St.
Raleigh, NC 27603
919.546.9282
www.frankharmon.com

FRANK HARMON, ARCHITECT
Architect: Frank Harmon
706 Mountford St.
Raleigh, NC 27603
919.829.9464
www.frankharmon.com

A Stream of One's Own

DESIGN WORKSHOP, INC.
Landscape Architect: Suzanne Richman
120 E. Main St.
Aspen, CO 81611
970.925.8354
www.designworkshop.com

LIPKIN WARNER DESIGN AND PLANNING
Architect: Michael Thompson, David Warner, AIA
23400 Two Rivers Rd., Suite 44
Basalt, CO 81621
970.927.8473
www.lipkinwarner.com

Shelter and Embrace

DESIGN WITH NATURE, LLC
Landscape Designer: Donna Bone
PO Box 7300
Tesuque, NM 87574
505.983.5633
www.designwithnatureltd.com

ROBIN GRAY ARCHITECTS LLC
Architect: Robin Gray
511 Agua Fria
Santa Fe, NM 87501
505.995.8411
www.robingray.net

Variations on a Theme

CHARLES M. MCCULLOCH, ARCHITECT
Landscape Architect: Charles McCulloch, ASLA
2927 Newbury St.
Berkley, CA 94703
510.548.3888
www.cmmcculloch.com

FOX DESIGN GROUP ARCHITECTS
Architect: Dennis Fox
116 Washington Ave., Suite D
Point Richmond, CA 94801
510.235.3369
www.foxdesigngroup.com

Japanese Journey

JULIE MOIR MESSERVY & ASSOCIATES, INC.
Landscape Designer: Julie Moir Messervy
Saxwin Building
18 Main St.
Saxtons River, VT 05154-0629
802.869.1470
www.juliemoirmesservy.com

HAMLIN & CO., INC.
Architect: Linda Hamlin
Contractor: David Hamlin
6 Wellington Terrace
Brookline, MA 02445
617.566.2161

Parallel Paths

ALCHEMIE
Landscape Architect: Bruce Hinckley
75 S. Main St. #313
Seattle, WA 98104
206.521.0358
www.alchemiesites.com

SUYAMA PETERSON DEGUCHI
Architect: George Suyama, FAIA
2324 Second Ave.
Seattle, WA 98121
206.256.0809
www.suyamapetersondeguchi.com

The Territory of Home

HORIUCHI SOLIEN INC.
Landscape Architect: Kris Horiuchi, ASLA
200 Main St.
Falmouth, MA 02540
508.540.5320
www.horiuchisolien.com

MARK HUTKER & ASSOCIATES ARCHITECTS INC.
Architect: Mark Hutker
79 Beach Rd.
Vineyard Haven, MA 02568
508.693.3344
217 Clinton Ave.
Falmouth, MA 02540
508.540.0048
www.hutkerarchitects.com

The World behind the Walls

JULIE MOIR MESSERVY & ASSOCIATES, INC.
Landscape Designer: Julie Moir Messervy
Saxwin Building
18 Main St.
Saxtons River, VT 05154-0629
802.869.1470
www.juliemoirmesservy.com

CAMPBELL-KING ASSOCIATES
Architect: Abigail Campbell-King, AIA
11 Friendship St.
Jamestown, RI 02835
401.423.3321

Living Lightly on the Land

KINGS CREEK MANAGEMENT, INC.
Landscape Designer: Jon Ahreus
3901-A Spicewood Springs Rd., Suite 201
Austin, TX 78759
512.615.2775
www.kingscreeklandscaping.net

MAIER + ZELTER ARCHITECTS
Architects: John Maier, AIA, Ulrike Zelter
5808 Balcones Dr., Suite 204
Austin, TX 78731
512.450.0121
www.maierzelter.com

Easy Living

SITEWORKS DESIGN GROUP, LLC
Landscape Architect: Cally Heppner, ASLA
24 Market
Beaufort, SC 29906
843.846.2259

YESTERMORROW, LLC
Architect: Ken Troupe
24 Market
Beaufort, SC 29906
843.846.0100
www.yestermorrow.net

A Landscape of Stone

LAURA GIBSON, ASLA
Landscape Designer: Laura Gibson
Manchester, MA 01944
978.526.8790
www.lgld.com

ROBINSON + GRISARU ARCHITECTURE PC
Architect: Richard Grisaru, Gitta Robinson
55 Washington St., Suite 711
Brooklyn, NY 11201
718.923.0040
www.rgarch.com

Good Fences

CLINTON & ASSOCIATES, LANDSCAPE ARCHITECTS
Landscape Architect:
Sandra Youssef Clinton, ASLA
5200 Baltimore Ave., Suite 201
Hyattsville, MD 20781
301.699.5600
www.clinton-la.com

Rooms Inside and Out

KOLLER AND ASSOCIATES
Landscape Designer: Gary L. Koller
993 Park St.
Stoughton, MA 02072
617.448.7247

Garden of Earthly Delights

ROSALIND REED ASSOCIATES
Landscape Designer: Rosalind Reed, APLD
529 North Grove
Oak Park, IL 60302
708.524.3323
www.rosalindreed.com

PAUL BERGER & ASSOCIATES
Architect: Paul Berger
20 E. Cedar, Suite 16C
Chicago, IL 60611
312.664.0640
www.pbadesign.com

Three Cabins in a Forest

LINDA ATTAWAY LANDSCAPE ARCHITECTURE
Landscape Architect: Linda Attaway
1402 Third Ave., Suite 800
Seattle, WA 98101
206.838.4110

CUTLER ANDERSON ARCHITECTS
Architect: Jim Cutler
135 Parfitt Way SW
Bainbridge Island, WA 98110
206.842.4710
www.cutler-anderson.com

At Home on the Range

DESIGN WORKSHOP, INC.
Landscape Architect: Richard Shaw, FASLA
120 E. Main St.
Aspen, CO 81611
970.925.8354
www.designworkshop.com

CCY ARCHITECTS
Architect: Larry Yaw, FAIA
PO Box 529
Basalt, CO 81621
970.927.4925
www.ccyarchitects.com

Terraces of Grass

SCOTT SHANNON, LANDSCAPE ARCHITECT
Landscape Architect: Scott Shannon, ASLA
Architect: Scott Shannon
5 Emory Ave.
Cazenovia, NY 13035
315.470.6537

A Cottage in the City

AMORY ARCHITECTS
Garden Designer: Sukie Amory
Architect: David Linzee Amory, AIA
7 Harvard Square
Brookline, MA 02445
617.277.4111
www.amoryarchitects.com